Tower Bridge

Tower Bridge

HONOR GODFREY

John Murray

For
my father

© Honor Godfrey 1988

First published 1988
by John Murray (Publishers) Ltd
50 Albermarle Street, London W1X 4BD

Reprinted 1991

Printed in Great Britain by Butler & Tanner Ltd,
Frome and London

British Library Cataloguing in Publication Data

Godfrey, Honor
Tower Bridge,
1. London. Road bridges: Tower Bridge,
to, 1985
I. Title
624'.82094215

ISBN 0-7195-4536-6

Frontispiece: Tower Bridge
from the east, 1964.

Contents

Acknowledgements

This book has been five years in the writing, and I owe initial gratitude to the Robin Wade & Pat Read Design Partnership for interesting me in the bridge, and to the City Engineer, Len Groome, for giving the project his blessing.

In the course of my research, I have received help, time, and encouragement from numerous people. At the Corporation of London, I wish to thank Betty Masters, formerly Keeper of the Records, James Sewell, Keeper of the Records, and Ralph Hyde, Keeper of Prints and Maps. At the bridge, my thanks are due to former Bridge Master, Commander Tony Rabbit, his successor, Colonel Roy Dalton, and the Tourist Manager, Mark Waters. I am indebted to Irene Peach for lending me family papers relating to the architect George Stevenson, to Dr Rowan Francis for his welcome at the Forncett Industrial Steam Museum, Norfolk, and to Avril Jones for her enlightening guided tour of Docklands. To friends who have contributed anecdotes, ephemera, and photographs, especial thanks: Moira Black and Robert Gurd, Richard Perfitt, Robert Opie, Dilwyn Chambers, Bill Wright, Jill Harmsworth, and Steve Morrissey. To those who have read — and perceptively commented on — the text, my grateful appreciation: Robert Scully, Sally Rousham, Peter Jackson, and Pedro Pra-Lopez.

Finally, I thank my father, Bernard Godfrey, for his continued support, my husband, David McCabe, for his lasting patience, and my editor and friend, Caroline Davidson, for her faith in the endeavour.

I

The Wonder Bridge of London

Oh, cloud capt towers! Oh, spanking spans!
What is it here I see?

(Old Father Thames, 'Our Giant Causeway', *Punch*, 30 June 1894)

As THE GREAT bascules moved slowly upwards, the waiting crowds that thronged the River Thames burst forth in jubilant cheers and applause. Many had been waiting hours to witness this — the inauguration of London's newest bridge. On a glorious June day in 1894, the culmination of eight years' relentless labour was realized when the Prince of Wales declared Tower Bridge open for land and river traffic. Much needed and long overdue, the bridge epitomized the mechanical genius of the late nineteenth century. A remarkable feat in both engineering and architectural terms, it was yet another in the long line of bridge-building achievements that studded Queen Victoria's reign.

Initially, Tower Bridge was designed by the City Architect, Horace Jones, at the instigation of the Corporation of London. Unlike all other Thames bridges, it had to cater for the passage of tall-masted ships making their stately way to the quaysides of the Upper Pool. This meant either a moving bridge or one with an elevated roadway and appropriate approaches. With navigation rather than defence in mind, Jones proposed a fanciful Gothic drawbridge, an aesthetic gateway entrance to the capital. Subsequent changes to his design did not eliminate the concept, and Tower Bridge consists of a pair of opening leaves — or bascules — and two suspended spans connecting the main towers and the shores. The secret of the bascules (French *bascule*: see-saw) lies in their counterweighting, not essential in their medieval forebears, but greatly adding to their efficiency.

Watching the river pageant on Opening Day, 30 June 1894.

The name was first used in November 1872 when a bill seeking authority to build a 'tower bridge' was put before Parliament. Later, the Governor of the Tower of London was to apply to the Duke of Cambridge to have the name of the bridge changed by the Corporation to the Thames Bridge. Permission was never granted. The name, and the stipulation that the successful design was to be in keeping with the Tower of London, serve to convince many that the bridge has been there as long as its venerable neighbour.

Impetus for bridge-building in the nineteenth century was provided by the coming of the railways. The great weight of a steam train could not be borne by a slender cast-iron arch or suspension bridge, and new materials and methods of construction had to be found. Robert Stephenson's wrought-iron Britannia Bridge for the Chester-to-Holyhead railway over the Menai Strait was the boldest civil engineering achievement of the early Victorian era. Later in the century, the spectacular Forth Railway Bridge, still the longest railway bridge in the world and the first major bridge to be constructed of steel, enjoyed comparable success.

Iron in various forms had been known for many centuries, but the expense and unreliability of processing methods meant that it remained uncompetitive as a structural material until the Industrial Revolution. The first iron bridge was built across the Severn at Coalbrookdale in the West Midlands in 1779. During the nineteenth century, great strides were made in processing technology which continued to improve the quality, increase the availability, and lower the price of iron. In

William the Conqueror built the White Tower of the Tower of London. It predates Tower Bridge by eight centuries.

the 1830s and 1840s, large-scale iron and glass structures included vast greenhouses and railway train sheds. These were the forerunners of Paxton's Crystal Palace, built in Hyde Park, London, for the Great Exhibition of 1851. By the end of the 1850s, however, exposed ironwork and simple form were proving less acceptable to mainstream architectural opinion. Subsequent decades demanded first elaboration of Tower Bridge, open to shipping, in Mr Horace Jones's original design of 1878. Built of brick in medieval style, it was designed to harmonize with the Tower of London and 'might be rendered the most picturesque bridge on the river'. The bascules were to be raised and lowered with chains like an ancient drawbridge, the hoisting machinery worked 'by steam power or by hydraulic apparatus, supplied by tanks fixed in the roof of the towers'. The arched form of the steel girders did not allow the bascules to open fully and sailing-ships would have had great difficulty in keeping precisely to the centre of the opening.

structural iron and steel, then disguise. Tower Bridge, with its steel framework and masonry cladding, provides the ultimate late Victorian illustration of architectural icing on the structural cake.

This change in attitude may have arisen because of the division of labour between architect and engineer, which started on the railways. The great pioneer engineers of the first half of the century were either dead or retired by the end of the century, exhausted by their sole responsibility for works unprecedented in scale and magnitude. After 1850, works were no less spectacular but they lacked the human drama of one individual striving against the odds. There was a shift in the balance of power with architects in the ascendant and the great contractors stealing the limelight from the engineering consultants. Tower Bridge was designed, modified, and master-minded by an illustrious team of architects, engineers, and contractors of world-wide repute. It was they who drove the armies of building labourers and navigators or 'navvies' re-lentlessly on in the name of progress.

The length of Queen Victoria's reign was very much re-sponsible for the breadth of achievement. Buildings and civil-engineering works were regularly allocated by competition, the necessary finance raised by public subscription. On 18 December 1824, the earliest design for a bridge just east of the Tower of London, 'St. Catherine's Bridge of Suspension', was illustrated on the front page of *The Portfolio*. The bridge's promoters, Captain Samuel Brown and James Walker, proposed to raise the £392,000 deemed necessary by subscription, in transferable shares, of £100 each. They showed that tolls were likely to yield more than £100 per day and that investors might expect a 10 per cent return on their outlay. Sixty years on, however, the money for Tower Bridge was forthcoming from a source of great antiquity, the Bridge House Estates Trust. The Trust had its origins in the twelfth century, in the early days of Old London Bridge, when tolls, dues and rents, charitable donations, and bequests 'To God and the Bridge' went towards its upkeep and maintenance. Today, income from its property and funds is still used to maintain the four bridges owned by the Corporation of London — London, Southwark, Blackfriars, and Tower — at no expense to the ratepayer or taxpayer.

Up and down the country, monuments of every description were erected during Queen Victoria's long and distinguished

Progress on the bridge, one of a vigorous set of drawings by Henri Lanos for *The Graphic*, 4 June 1892.

4

TOWER BRIDGE *Lemonade Crystals*

EACH BOTTLE MAKES 2 GALLONS

A face-pack for the bridge by Messrs Pearce Duff, manufacturers of a celebrated brand of lemonade crystals.

reign. Some have gone, others still stand, and many have been relegated by time. The Victorians lavished praise and endless prose on their new building achievements, likening them to the Seven Wonders of the World, and extolling their virtues as monuments for posterity. Across the Atlantic, similar adulation was heaped on American structural feats. When the Brooklyn Bridge, linking Manhattan and Brooklyn over the East River, opened in 1883, it was compared to Babylon's hanging gardens, Nineveh's towers, and Rome's Colosseum, and *Harper's Weekly* found it 'more wonderful than the Pyramids'.

Contemporary criticism of Tower Bridge was mixed but rapidly swung in favour of popular acclaim. The bridge became the subject of innumerable paintings, engravings, etchings, and photographs, and featured in books and advertising. Its memorable outline ensured its use millions of times over to send 'Greetings from London'. As the river's most easterly bridge and its water-gate, it became inseparable from the mighty Thames, the very hub of trade and commerce. Like its contemporaries, the Eiffel Tower and the Statue of Liberty, it represented its capital to the world, its well-being deeply rooted in national consciousness.

The busy Thames captured on a promotional calendar for 1898.

6

"LONDONS WATER GATE" (THE TOWER BRIDGE)

FROM
WILLIAM KAY,
Tea Dealer and Provision Merchant,
MARKET PLACE, HOWDEN.

7

In under a century, Tower Bridge has assumed a world-wide significance out of all proportion to its age and standing. Why is it that a bridge, not the longest, the highest, or the greatest, has become one of the best-loved sights of London and an internationally recognized symbol? When it first opened, any consideration of Tower Bridge as a landmark was quite incidental to its prime function as a vital road and river crossing. In its heyday, the great hydraulic engines concealed in the piers of the two towers raised the twin bascules to shipping up to fifty times a day. However, as the twentieth century progressed, the commercial wharves upstream closed, and today the bridge, operated by electrical power, opens to river traffic but two or three times a week. Its original claim to fame has now been surpassed by its role as an historic monument and, most recently, as a major new tourist attraction open to the public.

In 1968, London Bridge was sold to the McCulloch Oil Corporation of Los Angeles. That the Americans thought they were buying Tower Bridge is a widely held popular belief but Tower Bridge is a British institution and one that is definitely here to stay.

II

A New River Crossing

A mighty edifice man's mind has planned,
By which a mighty river has been spanned.

(Memories of London, c. 1930)

FOR HUNDREDS OF years, London flourished with only one bridge across the Thames. Old London Bridge, built of stone, reached the height of its fame in Shakespeare's day, when it was justly regarded as one of the wonders of the world. 'Handsome and well-built houses...occupied by merchants of consequence' flanked the narrow thoroughfare, perpetually crammed with busy stalls, itinerant traders, carts, and droves of cattle. By 1750, London Bridge was living up to its nursery-rhyme namesake, its foundations shaky, its buildings tottering. John Rennie's replacement bridge, constructed alongside, was opened by King William IV in 1831, and the remnant of its historic predecessor demolished a year later. Putney Bridge was the second to be built — a wooden viaduct — in 1729. In the next hundred years, no less than eight bridges were constructed, catering largely for the fashionable coach-keeping élite and spurred on by the development of London south of the Thames.

When Queen Victoria came to the throne, London was all set to sprawl, the metropolis transformed by steam power and the unprecedented advances of the Industrial Revolution. Traffic was multiplying on the roads and the capital was about to be criss-crossed by railway lines. The first railway bridges paid scant regard to their well-conceived neighbours, spanning the Thames where it suited them, and providing many a blot aesthetically. Few complained, though John Ruskin left no doubt as to his feelings about Blackfriars Railway

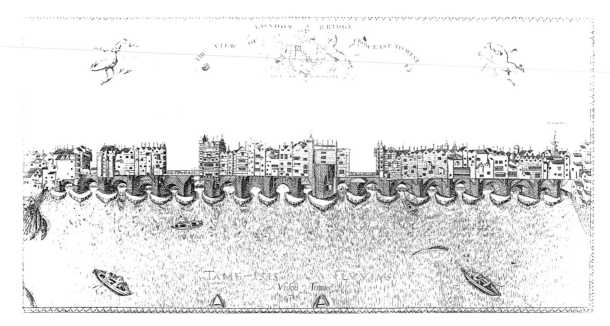

Bridge: 'The entire invention of the designer seems to have exhausted itself in exaggerating to an enormous size a weak form of iron nut, and in conveying the information upon it, in large letters, that it belongs to the London, Chatham & Dover Railway Company'.

As Victoria's reign unfolded, tunnels, subways, and bridges came thick and fast, each addition serving further to undermine the livelihoods of the Thames watermen. For generations, these men had fought competition from road transport, and readers of *The River Thames,* one of Nelson's 'Hand-Books for Tourists' published in 1859, knew their 'palmy days' were now over, 'since the erection of so many magnificent bridges' left them 'small service of their trade' and thinned their numbers 'in a lamentable degree'. But the second half of the nineteenth century was to be dominated by a debate that was to strike far deeper into the heart of the river, right into the 'myriad-masted bosom of the Thames'. The controversy raged over a proposed new crossing east of London Bridge which seemingly threatened a river full of shipping and the vested interests of the wharves on either side. Below London Bridge, continued the handbook, the 'vast thicket of shipping' constituted 'the wonder and glory of London' and stood for 'the commercial wants and enterprize of the world'. There was such a multitude of craft that 'with the exception of a narrow pathway in the centre, one might walk from deck to deck for

Old London Bridge in its heyday, engraved by John Norden, Royal Surveyor to Queen Elizabeth I, *c.*1600. The nineteen stone piers reduced the river to one-sixth of its normal flow and created a fall of water of up to 5 feet. The restriction of flow above the bridge meant that the river froze over in hard winters and ice fairs were held.

many a mile'. The wharves and quays which lined the banks were 'scarcely to be estimated for importance and extent. No river in the world can show anything equal to them'. The same was said of the docks, commensurate in size with the immense business carried out and with the value represented.

By the 1870s, a million people lived east of London Bridge, their only roadway across the Thames the bridge itself. Every day, thousands of pedestrians and horse-drawn wagons streamed westwards. In 1884, the House of Commons Select Committee on the Tower Bridge Bill heard that small rowing-boats were the only other means of communication between populations which had sprung up 'on the one side as large as Liverpool, and on the other side as large as Manchester, Salford and Birmingham combined'. Some relief had been provided in 1843 when the Thames Tunnel between Wapping and Rother-hithe opened. Built by the Brunels, Marc and his son Isambard, it was a truly remarkable feat of engineering. However, the novelty wore off, the tunnel degenerated, and in 1865 the East London Railway Company stepped in and began to use the tunnel for trains from Liverpool Street Station to the south coast. In 1871, the Tower Subway opened, just a little to the west of the future site of Tower Bridge. Soon a million people

The tumult on London Bridge captured in 'A London May Day', c.1870.

11

a year were crossing via the circular iron tube, at a halfpenny toll. (The subway was closed when the bridge opened and today carries public utilities under the river.)

Nevertheless, pressure was mounting for a new bridge to be built near or east of the Tower of London. Who would be responsible, the Corporation of London or the Metropolitan Board of Works? Both were being inundated with petitions and urgent representations from influential bodies. The Corporation asked the Bridge House Estates Committee and, on 10 February 1876, a special bridge or subway committee was set up 'to consider, and to report as to the desirability of erecting a bridge across, or a subway under the Thames east of London Bridge, and the best means of carrying out the same'. By the end of the year, it had concluded that the project should go ahead on a site from Little Tower Hill and Irongate Stairs on the north side to just to the west of Horselydown Lane and Stairs on the south side. Designs were now invited.

The Thames Tunnel took just over eighteen years to build by revolutionary new boring methods. A financial flop, there was never enough money to realize the 'Great Descents' for carriages so it became a tunnel for pedestrians (toll 1d.). The public flocked to walk beneath the waters of the Thames and to attend bazaars and illuminated fêtes held underground.

There was almost no end to the suggestions put forward — high-level bridges with inclined roadways and lifts, low-level bridges with openings or fixed roads, grand tunnels, complicated duplex and rolling bridges, and subways and ferries.

The Tower Subway under construction: it had an internal diameter of only 7 feet.

(below) Mr F. J. Palmer popularized his ideas for dealing with Thames floods and the relief of London Bridge in an illustrated pamphlet aimed at 'the Angler, Tourist and Boating Man'. In 1877, he proposed a 'duplex' bridge where vehicles would use alternate sections of the approach loop as vessels passed through the sliding sections. But the scheme was too complex and the available space too small for it to work.

(above) Grand tunnel entrance to a 'sub-riverian arcade', resting on the bed of the Thames, proposed by Mr John Keith in 1876.

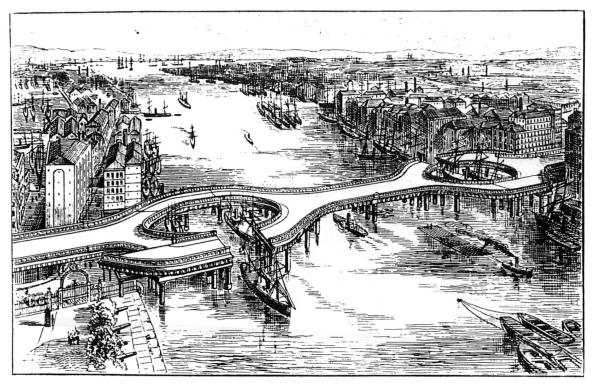

It was at a meeting in October 1878 that Mr Horace Jones was called upon to comment on the scheme submitted by Sir Joseph Bazalgette, the engineer to the Metropolitan Board of Works. Doubtless the authorities had hoped they would collaborate but Jones reported that 'Sir Joseph Bazalgette did not propose or desire to pursue the subject jointly with me'. He found that Bazalgette's high-level bridge scheme ignored 'the evidence, views, wishes and interests of the wharfingers and shipowners'. Mr H. A. Isaacs, Chairman of the Special Bridge Committee, went further in a letter to *The Times*: 'there was something very nearly approaching a consensus of opinion in condemnation of the bridge proposed by Sir Joseph Bazalgette'. 'Aquarius' directed his publication, 'The Tower (High Level)? Bridge. An Imperial Question', solely against Bazalgette: 'He, indeed, as will appear hereafter, is anxious to follow on with three more [schemes]. It is for the public to say whether it has sufficient appetite to swallow one'.

At the same time, Horace Jones produced his own plan for a low-level bridge on the bascule principle. Years later, he was to say in his evidence to the Select Committee that the sketches of the bridge, open and shut, were 'hasty', and that

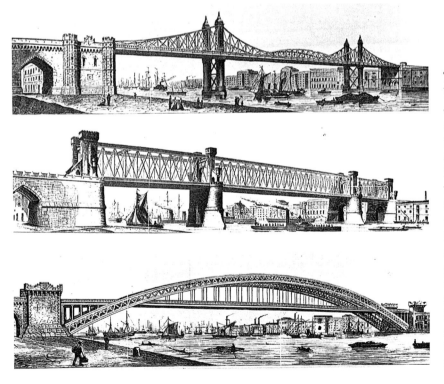

Three of Sir Joseph Bazalgette's disputed designs, all dating from 1878 and using the same basic plan and approach level. Headway for passing vessels was quite inadequate and the approaches would have had to be very long to achieve an easy gradient. Bazalgette was to reach the zenith of his career as a bridge designer a decade later with Hammersmith, Putney, and Battersea Bridges.

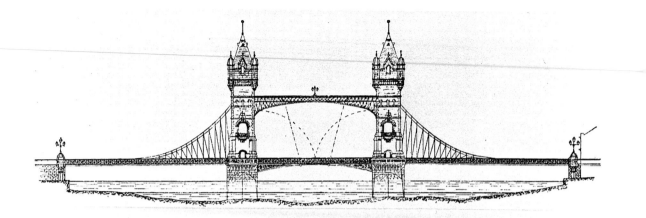

the scheme was a 'very crude notion'. Nevertheless, the concept was there and, though no proposals were adopted, the design was recommended. As an alternative, Jones was collaborating with Charles Gregory, a past President of the Institution of Civil Engineers, on a plan to widen London Bridge. Supporters of the new crossing, Webb and Bolland, damned this 'temporary and doubtful expedient' in their publication of 1877, 'Shall London Bridge be widened or shall a new bridge be built near the Tower?' If, according to the authors, the 'wealthiest city in the world' postponed building a new bridge, it would give rise to 'a humiliating spectacle for ourselves, and a cause of wonder to all civilized nations'.

Jones's bascule scheme lay dormant while bills for every means of communication, 'lifting, sliding, shooting and sinking', went before Parliament. In 1883, the London Chamber of Commerce offered to exhibit any maps, plans, or models of proposed schemes in its council rooms. Eleven designs were entered but none was taken up. Two of the more elaborate were Messrs Maynard and Cooke's high-level tunnel and Mr Guthrie's steam ford.

Finally, matters came to a head in 1884 when a select committee of the House of Commons sat for twenty-five days dealing with the whole question of Thames communications. A deputation from the Bridge House Estates Committee went on a trip to the Continent to inspect low-level bridges with mechanical openings. Horace Jones resurrected his bascule bridge idea and consulted the eminent engineer, John Wolfe Barry. The two men got on well and presented a joint design in October. Preparation of the necessary Parliamentary bill

The joint design submitted by Jones and Barry for Parliamentary approval in 1884. The most obvious change was the substitution of the straight span for Jones's arch so that the bascules could open vertically to give a 200-foot clearway. Pedestrian walkways were now a possibility at a high level.

was swift, but there were another nineteen days of evidence to be sifted, when the architectural, structural, and engineering details of the bridge, as well as its working, were carefully gone into. Barry made it known that he had consulted six or seven engineers of repute and 'therefore the bridge that is now before the Committee is not merely Mr Jones's and my proposal, but it is a proposal that before it took any tangible shape was endorsed by all those gentlemen'. Asked if he could stake his reputation on 'Mr Jones's flaps or wings' always opening at the right moment and at the requisite speed, he replied: 'If I was not convinced in my own mind that this was a thoroughly workable scheme, I am quite sure I

Letter from Henry Marc Brunel, John Wolfe Barry's partner, to his friend and business associate the hydraulic engineer, John George Gamble, 1 February 1885. Brunel was to supervise all the complicated calculations and details of the structure.

should not be sitting in this chair'. It was in the Lords that provision was made for compensation to be paid in the event of any loss arising from the new bridge. At last, on 14 August 1885, 'an Act to empower the Corporation of London to construct a bridge over the river Thames near the Tower of London, with approaches thereto', received the Royal assent.

Congratulations were now in order. Summing up to the Select Committee, Mr R.D.M. Littler, QC, said: 'That the scheme will be an enormous public advantage I think can hardly be denied; that the design is ornamentally satisfactory, I think, can hardly be denied. It is intended to be to a certain extent in harmony with the buildings of the Tower; it is intended to be an ornament to the river and it is intended to be provided without taxing anybody to the extent of a single halfpenny, which is a very large element in these days of large local and Imperial taxation. In point of fact, just as the City of London have made a present to the metropolis of its grandest park, that of Epping Forest, they are now prepared to make a present to the metropolis of another bridge, which, while not forgetting London Bridge, will be its most important and most valuable bridge'.

III

'The Leaders of the Enterprise'

And all the audacity of the modern architects, which is to create the works of the future, here bursts forth, suspended on the heavy foundations of the past, with so much measure and proportion that nothing offends in the medley of archaism and modernity.

THE POST OF Architect and Surveyor to the City of London Corporation was an ancient and prestigious one whose origins went back to the fifteenth-century office of Clerk of the Works. When Horace Jones was appointed in 1864, no other candidate could present so professional a case or such influential referees. With Cardiff 'Old' Town Hall, London office buildings, and a planned extension to the West End store Marshall & Snelgrove to his name, he already had some remarkable public and commercial structures behind him. Amongst other work for the City Corporation, he was to make numerous additions to the Guildhall, and to design the great City markets of Smithfield, Billingsgate, and Leadenhall, as well as Tower Bridge.

Jones's integrity as an official of the Corporation was nigh on legendary. Nevertheless, he was closely questioned about the professional ethics of presenting his own scheme for a Tower Bridge. In his evidence to the House of Commons Select Committee, he said: 'Do not suppose that I at all put this forward as my own design. It is rather an accumulation of ideas from a variety of other persons. It is done rather with the purpose of meeting the views of the Bridge House Committee than from any desire to push my design before the public'.

Whether Tower Bridge came fairly within the terms of Jones's

19

Horace Jones (1819–97), the City Architect. After the portrait in oils by W.W.Ouless, exhibited at the Royal Academy Summer Exhibition in 1887.

appointment was another debatable point. After all, London Bridge had been rebuilt by Sir John Rennie, Blackfriars by Mr Joseph Cubitt — both men specially appointed — and not by the City Architect. But since Jones had prepared the scheme, the Bridge House Estates Committee decided that he should be appointed architect for the erection and construction, particularly as he was in any case going to have to deal with 'all matters connected with the taking of property for the purpose of the proposed Bridge and its approaches', tasks which certainly fell within the duties of his office.

Horace Jones never saw Tower Bridge: he died quite suddenly in May 1887 before even the foundations were complete. But in John Wolfe Barry he had found a collaborator who would see the scheme through all its vicissitudes to completion. And changes there certainly were: the finished bridge was decidedly a variation on the Parliamentary approved theme.

Barry emerged from a family of architects as an engineer. His father, Sir Charles, designed the Houses of Parliament, while his elder brothers, Charles and Edward, were responsible between them for such notable buildings as Dulwich College, the Charing Cross Hotel, the Royal Opera House, and Floral Hall in Covent Garden. Barry's first job was as assistant engineer to the Charing Cross Railway. In 1867, he set up his own practice, concentrating particularly on railways, bridges, and docks, and by the turn of the century had become the acknowledged head of the engineering profession in Britain. While working as consulting engineer to Tower Bridge, he was also carrying out the Barry Dock near Cardiff (the largest single dock in the United Kingdom) and contributing to government commissions on Scottish and Irish public works, and on the Suez Canal.

Though Barry assumed full responsibility for the fledgling bridge after Jones's death, the architect George Stevenson was to have a major influence on its final appearance. Stevenson, who had been Jones's assistant, now set up in business on his own in King Street, Cheapside, where he strove for seven long years 'to perfect the design and modify the work, so as to adapt the buildings to the altered requirements of the engineer'. It has been said that he would not make a start before his choice of a stone facing in preference to the red bricks proposed by Jones had been approved.

Though the metal construction of Tower Bridge is fully clad

General view of the completed Tower Bridge. Mr Tuit, engineer to the contractors Sir William Arrol & Co., wrote in his account of the bridge in 1894: 'It will be seen that the present design differs in several important particulars, both of an engineering and architectural character, from the joint design laid before Parliament. Though Mr Barry has aimed at preserving the general appearance of the structure, he adopted a somewhat severer form of architecture for the main towers, while the chains, braced, and raised at the abutments, and the abutment towers themselves are altogether new features'.

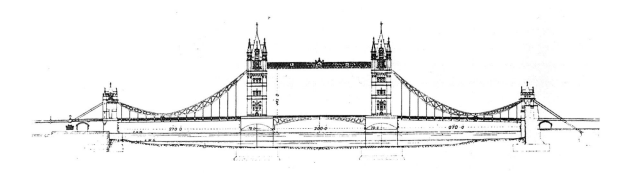

in line with late Victorian practice, the constraints of the framework, particularly the moving parts, left the architect with anything but a free hand. Iron had been a novel and daring constructional material at the start of Queen Victoria's reign, widely used for prefabricated buildings at home and abroad. Theatres, whole houses, and even shopping parades were shipped to the far-flung outposts of the Empire. But the association of iron with cheap utilitarian buildings grew and it became fashionable to disguise the structure with architectural cladding and decoration. The same went for steel, a stronger, more durable, and cheaper material than wrought iron. The age of bulk manufacture had arrived in 1856 when Henry Bessemer's new steel-making furnace provided up to 25 tons in half an hour. The construction of the mighty Forth Bridge between 1883 and 1890 virtually coincided with the almost total eclipse of cast and wrought iron and would have been impossible without steel. For the contractor, William Arrol, the Forth Bridge was the high point of a distinguished career and, as a result, *The Graphic* could report in 1894 that his firm was 'engaged in gigantic enterprises throughout the world'. Not that he was working on this one scheme

(left) George Daniel Stevenson (1846–1931), architectural assistant to Horace Jones, and later architectural consultant for the bridge.

(right) John Wolfe Barry (1837–1918), engineer-in-chief, knighted 1897. In 1898, he adopted the surname Wolfe-Barry.

alone: he was also the contractor for the new Tay Bridge (opened in 1887), Tower Bridge, and the far-distant Hawkesbury River Bridge in New South Wales. Much of his life was spent in trains, travelling from his Glasgow works to Edinburgh for the Forth Bridge, to Dundee for the Tay Bridge, and on overnight sleepers to London for weekend site meetings at Tower Bridge.

Arrol's Dalmarnock Works, established in 1872, were far from typical. Most manufactories at this stage were dark and dismal sheds, dimly lit by candles or gas lamps. His huge steel-framed workshops had roofs of steel and glass through which the daylight flooded. Here steelwork was prefabricated and trial erections took place. In 1875, Arrol had invented a riveting machine worked by hydraulic pressure which ensured absolute contact at all points of the riveted surfaces and perfect filling of holes by the stem of the rivet. Arrol's attention to detail extended to the well-being of his men. At the Forth Bridge, he put up rows of cottages, organized a sick club, dining-room, and reading-room, and issued protective clothing. He realized that the majority of accidents were due to preventable causes, to stages cluttered with litter, tools, rubbish, hammers, chisels, and wood, so he employed special gangs to clear up. Many of the lessons he learned were applied at Tower Bridge so that *The Times* could report: 'The experience gained by the contractors in constructing the Forth Bridge has been most valuable, and the impress of that work may be seen in many of the operations'.

Horace Jones had been an inveterate traveller who toured and studied extensively on the Continent. He had seen swing and vertical-lift bridges in Holland and Belgium where they had been part of the canal-rich landscape since the eighteenth century. An accomplished draughtsman and water-colourist, he had noted architectural styles and details during his travels. *The Builder* commented that 'though hardly what would now be called an "art architect", the late Sir Horace Jones had a good deal more perception as to the artistic element in architectural design than would be quite realised by those who knew him only as the architect of the City markets'.

When Jones first proposed an opening bridge, there was, according to Barry, 'some outcry by aesthetical people lest it should ruin the picturesqueness of the Tower of London by hideous girder erections, and it seems to be the universal wish that this bridge should be in harmony architecturally

William Arrol (1839–1913), steel-maker and contractor, knighted at the opening of the Forth Bridge, 4 March 1890.

with the Tower'. Jones chose the Scottish Baronial style as his medievalizing influence. *The Builder* described his design for the towers as 'a simple and somewhat impressive one, with a corbelled-out upper storey and angle-turrets somewhat after the manner of Scotch Castellated Gothic, and a band of panelling a little way below them, the rest of the tower being very simply treated'. Nevertheless, he captured the Crusader's castle and ensured a romantic silhouette by his use of high pitched roofs, interrupted by small windows and crowned with ornament.

In his 'Description of the Tower Bridge, its Design and Construction', Barry could see two possible ways of enclosing the steelwork, either cast-iron panelling or stone. Both would hide the constructive features equally well but stone would, of course, look better and 'practically speaking it is also better, when it is considered that there is no mode so satisfactory for preserving iron and steel from corrosion as embedding it in brickwork, concrete or masonry'. He feared that 'some purists will say that the lamp of truth has been sadly neglected in this combination of materials' but he hoped that 'we may forget that the towers have skeletons as much concealed as that of the human body, of which we do not think when we contemplate examples of manly or feminine beauty'.

The main erecting shop at the Dalmarnock Works, *c.*1909. There were four other erecting departments, as well as the pattern, joinery, and template shops.

24

Riveting at Dalmarnock, c.1909. 'The girder, or other piece of constructional work, when riveted up so far as can be done at the Works, is painted or oiled, and marked for erection purposes'.

It was now up to Stevenson to produce the necessary designs. His drawings are the painstaking masterpieces so characteristic of the Victorian architect's office, executed in ink and water-colour, and meticulous in every detail. Many are preserved in the Guildhall, including those found under the floor of his last house at Alexandra Palace. Only Stevenson's signature appears but he did apparently have some help from an assistant, Mr W.T. Hanman. The drawings reveal Stevenson's passion for all-over visual interest. He brought down the angle-turrets, exaggerated the fanciful skyline, provided strong horizontal lines, and fitted in as many windows as he possibly could. He livened up the façades with elaborate window frames, balconies, and niches. He wove intricate patterns into the cast iron and let not one symbol of the endeavour go unmoulded in one material or another. Truly, it was to be the ultimate monument to High Victorian Gothic.

So much for the eminent professional 'leaders of the enterprise', hailed thus on opening day by the *Illustrated London News*. It was the Bridge House Estates Trust that financed the operation and took ultimate responsibility for making Tower Bridge happen. Over the years, its affairs had flourished, and during the nineteenth century the City of London Corporation, as trustees of the Fund, were able to spend a staggering £3¼ million on bridges across the Thames. This allowed the Corporation to 'rebuild, entirely free of cost to the ratepayers, London Bridge and Blackfriars Bridge, and to purchase and free from toll Southwark Bridge' as well as to erect Tower Bridge.

Barry estimated that the bridge would cost £585,000, plus £165,000 for the approaches, making a grand total of £¾ million. This the Corporation could borrow on the credit of the Bridge House Estates. Barry asked for the usual commission — £5 per cent on the Parliamentary estimate for the bridge of £610,000 — to be shared between himself and Jones. This led to considerable debate, as reported by the Bridge House Estates Committee to the Court of Common Council on 23 October 1886. It was argued that Horace Jones's duties in connection with the bridge were part of his responsibilities as City Architect for which 'he already received a handsome salary'. It was also felt that a lesser commission should have satisfied 'the most eminent engineer of the day'. Eventually, it was agreed that 'the sum of £30,000 should be paid to Mr Architect and Mr Barry in such proportions as they may mutually agree upon for their services in respect thereof'. On 24 December, *The Architect* summarized the agreement in detail. Jones and Barry were to 'direct, manage and superintend the works..., to design all works and prepare all plans, specifications, and drawings..., to settle...the details of all contracts..., to provide and pay for all superintendents, clerks of the works, inspectors and assistants..., to examine all materials to be used in construction..., to check all work, accounts, bills, etc., and to perform all duties and services of architect and engineer in relation to the bridge, apportioning the duties between them, but each to be responsible to the Corporation for the whole'. The Corporation had the power to revoke the appointment of either and 'provisions are also made in case of the death of either gentleman or their disagreement'.

For the steelwork, Arrol's received £337,113, and Sir William G. Armstrong, Mitchell & Co. Ltd., who were responsible for the hydraulic machinery, £85,232. The piers and abutments cost nearly as much as the masonry superstructure, £131,344 as opposed to £149,122.

When the final day of reckoning came, however, the bridge had cost over £1 million.

IV

Building Tower Bridge

*The most monumental example of extravagance in bridge
construction in the world...*

(Waddell, quoted in *The Guinness Book of Structures*)

ON 14 AUGUST 1885, the Corporation of London (Tower
Bridge) Act received the Royal assent. The Corporation was
given four years to build the bridge and its approaches but
delays and difficulties meant that two time extensions were
required and it was to be eight years before the task was
finished. Meanwhile 'the progress was watched with much
interest by the public from London Bridge'.

John Jackson of Westminster was the successful tenderer for
the abutments and foundations of the two river piers. He had
set up as an engineering contractor in Newcastle in 1876 and
had quickly made his name with a succession of dock contracts
in Glasgow and the North-east. Actual work on Tower Bridge
began on 22 April 1886 and it was not long before Jackson
was involved in additional labour and expenditure in connection with the laying of the Memorial Stone on 21 June.
This ceremony took place on 'the first day of the fiftieth year
of Her Majesty's happy and prosperous reign' and was performed by the Prince of Wales on behalf of Queen Victoria.

Along the processional route from Marlborough House to
the Tower, there was a colourful display of flags and hangings,
and crowds of waiting spectators cheered the Royal carriages
as they passed. In a special pavilion erected on the Tower
waterfront and decked with gold and crimson, 1,500 people
were entertained by the Band of the Coldstream Guards and a
choir of 'lady pupils' from the Guildhall School of Music.
Guests included officers of the Corporation, members of the
Houses of Parliament and prominent City figures, as well as

The Prince laying the Memorial Stone. In reply to the Recorder's address on behalf of the Corporation, he said: 'It gives the Princess of Wales and myself sincere pleasure to be permitted, on behalf of the Queen, my dear mother, to lay the first stone of the new Tower Bridge, and in her name we thank you for your loyal address, and assure you of her interest in this great undertaking'.

200 visitors from India and the colonies, in London for the Colonial and Indian Exhibition. At 4 o'clock, the Prince of Wales daubed the Memorial Stone with mortar and it was lowered into position. In the cavity beneath was a time capsule — a vase containing papers and coins. The Bishop of London offered a short prayer, the Tower guns marked the auspicious occasion by the firing of a salute, and the Princess of Wales graciously accepted the emblem of the Bridge House Estates set in diamonds. As revealed later in the *Architect & Contract Reporter*, Horace Jones narrowly escaped death 'by the falling of a part of one of the machines in use' but lived to receive a knighthood in August. Photographs of the afternoon's events taken by the London Stereoscopic Company were a complete failure. They charged the Corporation ten guineas for their pains and attributed their lack of success to 'insurmountable difficulties in the way of our taking any better pictures, the day being dull, and the tent dark, and the crowding of people being so very great'.

The formal ceremony over, work could begin in earnest. The piers of the bridge are complicated structures, housing the counterpoise and machinery of the opening spans and supporting the towers carrying the suspension chains and high-level walkways. They are sunk into the underlying London clay to a depth of 25 feet and are of concrete below the river bed and of brick and granite above. Their foundations were dug out by teams of navvies working within a series of caissons.

The caissons were open-ended boxes of wrought iron with a sharp cutting edge at the bottom for penetrating the ground. There were twelve to each pier, formed approximately to the shape of the finished pier. Two and a half feet was left between them, the minimum space in which a man could work effectively. The caissons were erected *in situ* on timber staging and gradually lowered into the river. The lower part was permanent and the upper part temporary. The temporary caisson was simply to keep the water out while the pier was being built and the joint between the two was made tight with india-rubber. When the caisson was ready, the staging was removed and it was lowered by means of four powerful screws attached to four lowering rods. Divers working inside the caissons excavated first gravel, then the upper layers of the London clay, which were hauled up by crane and dumped into waiting barges. Once the caisson had reached the required depth, the space was pumped out and navvies were able to get to the bottom and dig out the clay in the dry. Additional temporary lengths were added as the caissons sank so that each was finally an iron box 57 feet high. All the permanent caissons and spaces between were then filled with concrete.

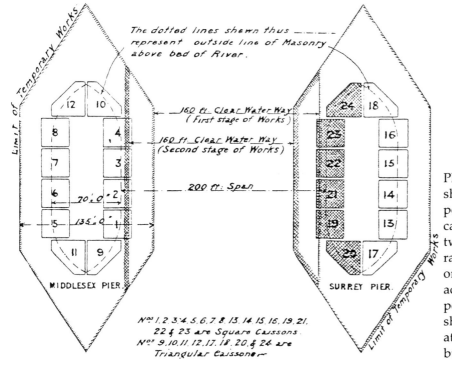

Plan of the piers showing the positioning of the caissons. By using twelve small caissons rather than one large one extending right across a pier, it was possible to work on the shore side of one pier at the same time as building the other.

The work was troublesome and tedious and took much longer than expected. The two piers could not be built at the same time because a clear 160-foot waterway had always to be maintained. Vessels had to remain shoreside so there was constant handling and rehandling of materials, plant, and waste when working riverside. The wooden staging looked big but was mostly occupied by large cranes which left little storage space. As a result, supplies had to be ordered piecemeal and delays in their delivery held up proceedings still further.

Jackson's contract took the piers to a height of 4 feet above high water and was not completed until January 1890. He was also responsible for the abutment piers which were built within coffer dams and 'though formidable in size and depth, presented no new features of construction'.

Eight months earlier, the contract for the construction and erection of the steelwork had been let to Arrol's. William Arrol, always personally involved, was aided on site by his engineer from Forth Bridge days, the 'kindly, able' Mr Tuit, and by John Hunter, his business representative. At the Dalmarnock Works, Mr Jackaman looked after Barry's interests by exercising quality control over the finished product. All

View of the piers under construction, showing the timber staging, cranes, and barges alongside.

'The Present State of the Tower Bridge — A View from the Tower Pier, Surrey Side' by Henri Lanos for *The Graphic*, 20 February 1892.

30

31

Progress on the upper walkways, March 1892.

the steelwork was made in the Glasgow neighbourhood, not only by Arrol's, but also by the Steel Company of Scotland, A. & J. Stewart, and Clydesdale. It was despatched to London by the steamers of the Clyde Shipping and Carron Companies and transferred to the contractor's barges within half a mile of the bridge. As much riveting as possible had already been done but the weight of each piece of steel was limited to about 5 tons for ease of handling. Anything urgently required was sent down by train.

Arrol's first problem was one of access, solved by building temporary bridges out from the shores to each pier. He also took over Jackson's timber staging as a further base from which to work. The steelwork of the main towers consists of octagonal columns in the four corners and three sets of horizontal landing girders with diagonal wind braces inserted between. The columns in their small pieces were lifted into position by crane and hand-riveted by squads of men standing on movable stages. A good squad was able to put in about two hundred $7/8$-inch rivets in a ten-hour day. As each landing was installed, so the cranes were moved up and the work continued. The wind bracing, either flat steel plates or curved struts, was again generally hand-riveted, though Arrol's special hinged hydraulic riveting machine was used wherever possible.

32

Constructing the main chains.

Work began on the steel columns of the abutment towers when the river towers were about half built. The columns, smaller in diameter, are connected by lattice bracing.

The two steel columns on the riverside support the high-level footways, the two on the shoreside take the weight of the chains. Each walkway is made up of three sections: cantilevers on either side and a central linking section. The cantilevers were built out length by length from each tower using cranes on the top landings and, later, small building cranes on travelling stages. The two halves of the middle girders were similarly constructed from either side until they met over the centre of the river. Accuracy was essential since the final length had already been made and tested at the trial erection of the walkways at the Dalmarnock Works.

The lower halves of the footway girders were plated over and ornamented with cast-iron mouldings and panelling. Cast-iron tracery filled the lattice bracing above. The roofs were of timber with a zinc covering and skylights at intervals. All the riveting and fixing was accomplished from a wooden stage attached to the underside of each footway. This was also needed to catch any rivets, bolts, or light tools that might fall into the river or on to vessels beneath. As Tuit commented: 'This last consideration was one of the greatest importance, as

the many pleasure steamers, crowded with passengers, continually passing under these footways necessitated the greatest care on the part of the contractors'.

Work begins on the girders of the bascules.

Building the chains was seen as the hardest part of the whole operation. Their weight — about 1 ton per foot run — meant that the trestles, designed to support them during erection and built on top of the temporary bridges, had to be extremely substantial and very well braced. A travelling gantry capable of carrying a steam crane was constructed in order to build those parts of the chains that cranes on the piers and abutments could not reach. Meanwhile, the land ties from the anchorages on either shore had been brought up to the tops of the abutment towers, and the horizontal ties, carried by the outer girders of the high-level walkways, had been erected and riveted in position. The ends of the ties and the junctions of the chains could now be bored and pinned together. At last there was a through connection from north to south bank. The chains are connected to the shore spans by suspension rods. These were not fixed until the roadway girders had been built and riveted on the temporary bridges and corrugated floor plates laid. The floor plates were then filled up with concrete and a road surface of wood paving blocks put down.

34

There are four main girders in each of the leaves of the opening span. The portions which would eventually be landward of the main pivots were constructed on the staging around the piers, raised to an upright position, and threaded with the pivot shafts. As the 160-foot clearway for shipping could never be obstructed, the girders had to be erected in the vertical. When lengths reaching about 40 feet over the central span had been built, the toothed quadrants which would work the bascules were constructed. None of the hydraulic machinery was installed at this stage so rotation of the moving girders in order to fit the teeth of the quadrants to those of the pinions was achieved by temporary means — a small steam winch. The whole 100-foot length of the girders was then completed. Not only the steelwork but also most of the paving was carried out when the bascules were raised. The Acme Flooring Company laid creosoted blocks of pine fixed one to another with oak dowels. They took the opportunity of running asphalt into the joints when the leaves were lowered for testing.

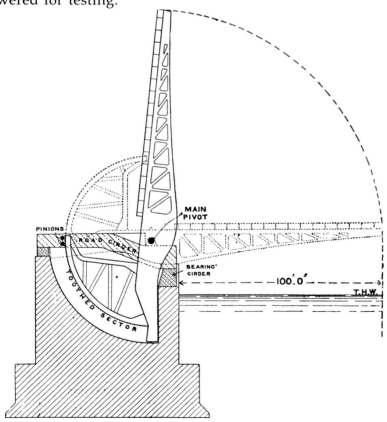

Diagram of a bascule, showing the main pivot, toothed quadrant, and pinions.

35

The most rigorous test was applied to the south bascule a few days before the bridge opened when a colossal weight of steam-rollers, traction engines, and trollies loaded with granite refuse was placed at its far extremity. According to the *St. James's Budget*, 'it must afford the greatest satisfaction to the engineer and contractors to know that the only deflection registered was the insignificant one of a trifle over 1½in'.

Responsibility for the masonry cladding was entrusted to Messrs Perry & Co. — now under the sole proprietorship of Herbert Bartlett — in May 1889. This large and successful building and construction firm specialized in hospitals, offices, hotels, and public buildings. Perry's work could only start when the steelwork of the towers was well under way and the firm had to make sure it did nothing to hold up general progress. Each tower is covered with a facing of grey granite and Portland stone, backed with brickwork. Had the walls been continuous from bottom to top, they would have had to be much thicker. As it is, the landing girders carry them from

'Testing the stability of the bridge', *St. James's Budget*, 29 June 1894. A weight of 150 tons, 'a greater weight than is ever likely to be upon the bascules again', was used to measure deflection.

floor to floor. Fears were voiced about expansion and contraction of the steelwork and its possible corrosion within the masonry cladding. As preventative measures, the steel columns were wrapped in oiled canvas as the masonry was built around them, and spaces were left where any subsequent compression might bring undue weight to bear on adjacent stonework. The columns were washed with neat cement as a protection against rust.

The granite came from the Eddystone granite quarries at De Lank, Cornwall. Each stone was cut and dressed to suit the position it was to occupy before it was shipped. Handwork was avoided by the use of Brunton & Trier's patent surfacing machines for plain work and their turning machines for circular and moulded work. The men worked on the masonry from stages which could be raised or lowered by wire ropes. Materials were moved by travelling steam cranes, placed on rails on the steelwork of the landings.

The two river towers are exactly the same. At each corner there is a circular turret containing the steel column. The four stages are divided by broad bands of plain masonry and accentuated by string courses above and below. The faces are ornamented with arched windows, bold mouldings, canopied niches, emblazoned shields, finials, buttresses, balconies, pinnacles, and parapets — the trappings of Victorian Gothic. The high pitched roofs, covered with Welsh slates, were crowned

The masonry work of the river towers nearing completion.

with elaborate open tracery, 19 feet in height.

The masonry of the abutment towers was built using the steam cranes and scaffolding when the steelwork was quite finished. The Middlesex tower is smaller than the Surrey one but they are both basically large ribbed arches, decorated with the arms of the City, parapets, and gargoyles, and topped by slate roofs with dormer windows and finials on the lead ridges. All the modelling and carving of the stone was carried out at the bridge, either on the ground or *in situ*, by Mabeys of Westminster.

The ornamental cast-iron parapets, and the decorative panels for the high-level walkways, were made by Messrs Fullerton, Hodgard, and Barclay, of Paisley. Both these and the lamp standards were designed by George Stevenson and fixed by W. Sugg & Co. of Westminster. Sugg's took a full page in the *Building News* on 29 June 1894 to announce that 'The Tower Bridge is lighted entirely by gas, by means of upwards of 200 Sugg's patent high-power flat-flame gas lamps'. Their adver-

Lamp standards on the northern approach.

'The Eve of Completion: Clearing away Scaffolding'. Another drawing by Lanos for *The Graphic*'s special supplement, 30 June 1894.

39

tisement continued: 'All the work of supplying and running gas and water mains, and supplying and fixing lamps, ornamental lamp standards and columns, hydrants, tanks, and hand pumps, wrought iron gates and railings has been carried out by William Sugg & Co.' As for the original colour of the bridge, Tuit stated that exposed steelwork 'received three finishing coats of paint of an approved quality, the last coat being bright chocolate in colour'.

Mr Cruttwell, the resident engineer, noted that on average 432 men were employed during the eight-year building period. Reports on loss of life during construction vary. Barry said six men died 'and at least one of these was the result of sudden illness, or of a fit'. Cruttwell gave a total of ten, four in sinking the foundations, one on the approaches, and the remaining five on the superstructure. Both were agreed, however, that the figures were low considering the magnitude and nature of the works.

Cruttwell read two papers on the building of the bridge to the Institution of Civil Engineers. The second, on the superstructure, was given in November 1896, the first year Barry was President of the Institution and, most opportunely, in the chair. Barry's own lecture was composed in 1893 and published the year after. Mr Tuit's contribution was an illustrated account, 'The Tower Bridge, its History and Construction, from the Date of the Earliest Project to the Present Time', published by *The Engineer* in 1894. The London illustrated journals as well as the engineering and architectural press avidly charted the progress of the new bridge, their enthusiasm mounting as the 'eve of completion' drew nigh.

George Edward Wilson Cruttwell, depicted in *The Graphic*, 30 June 1894, 'in the costume in which he superintended the laying of the foundations of the bridge'. He was resident engineer throughout, 'a patient, watchful man, who has borne a heavy responsibility well for the last eight years'.

V

'How it is Worked by the Moving of a Lever'

Nothing in their way at all equal to them [the bascules] is to be seen anywhere in the world, and to be near them in action is to witness one of the most imposing displays of hydraulic power that even Sir William Armstrong and his company have ever yet afforded.

(Architect & Contract Reporter, 6 July 1894).

FOR OVER EIGHTY years, Tower Bridge was operated by hydraulic power. The machinery, which was universally admired, was installed by Sir William G. Armstrong, Mitchell & Co. Ltd., the great nineteenth-century leaders in everything hydraulic. Provision of power was lavish but the large reserve always available meant that the machinery was never under stress and contributed to its faultless performance.

William Armstrong hailed from Newcastle and was an extraordinary man — lawyer, inventor, scientist, armaments' manufacturer, and shipbuilder. He invented hydraulic machinery of every description, including pit-winding engines, lifts, capstans, lock-gates, swingbridges, and drawbridges. Early on, large orders for his hydraulic crane, patented in 1846, meant that he could give up his first career of law and build his own works on the Tyne above Newcastle at Elswick. Thereafter his success as a hydraulic engineer stemmed from his use of water as a means of distribution rather than simply as a source of energy. In 1851, he built his first weight-loaded accumulator which could store power until such time as it was required. Seven years later, Armstrong himself was to write that this 'removed all obstacles to the extension of water pressure machinery, which has since been applied in nearly all the principal docks, and in many of the government

41

establishments in the country. The system has also been adopted in many of the principal railway stations, not only for cranage, but also for working turntables, traversing machines, wagon lifts, hauling machines etc. It is also extensively used for raising and tipping wagons in the shipment of coal, for opening and closing swing bridges and for many other purposes'.

In 1854, with Britain at war in the Crimea, Armstrong became interested in the production of weapons. He made a second and larger fortune from his breech-loaders and ironclads until by the time of his death in 1900 his firm vied with Krupps for the position of largest armaments' manufacturer in the world. He was 76 when Tower Bridge opened, and by then Lord Armstrong. A friend of royalty and foreign potentates, he entertained in the home he had had built perched high on the cliffs at Cragside, near Rothbury, Northumberland. Joseph Swan, the pioneer of electricity, was a friend and fellow Newcastle man, and Cragside was the first private house to be properly fitted with electric light. There were hydraulically operated embellishments too: the passenger lift, the kitchen spit, and the central heating. Even the heavy pots in the conservatories could be moved by hydraulic machinery.

Within a few decades, hydraulic power had become commonplace. By the end of the nineteenth century, most major

'The WONDER BRIDGE of LONDON and HOW it is WORKED by the MOVING of a LEVER', from *This and That*, November 1930.

cities had public hydraulic power supply companies with hydraulic mains providing power for cranes, dock gates, and passenger and goods lifts, at rates which were often more favourable than electricity. Hydraulic machinery was coming into use in the average metal shop for flanging and plate-bending presses, for riveting, punching, and drilling machines. It was William Arrol who developed the application of hydraulic machinery in construction work to its peak with hydraulic presses, multiple hydraulic drilling machines, and steam-driven pumps. At the Forth Bridge, his navvies used hydraulically operated spades to excavate the foundations.

The hydraulic machinery for Tower Bridge was designed by Armstrongs in conjunction with Barry, and presumably Brunel, who over twenty years earlier had served an apprenticeship at Elswick. (An Armstrong training was much coveted and Brunel was taken on when his family was in straitened circumstances after the commercial failure of the SS *Great Eastern*.) The machinery was constructed at the Elswick Works and erected on site by John Gass under the supervision of Samuel George Homfray of Armstrongs. It occupied the engine house in the arches under the southern approach and the machinery chambers in the two piers. Because of the recent Tay Bridge disaster, the Board of Trade required that all bridges be designed to withstand the very high wind pressure of 56lb. per sq. ft. (87 m.p.h.). In fact, all the machinery at Tower Bridge was duplicated which meant in effect that the provision of power was equal to *twice* the requirements of the Board of Trade.

When most of the Tay Bridge and a passenger train disappeared into the icy waters of the Firth in December 1879, it was generally agreed that 'what caused the overthrow of the bridge was the pressure of wind acting upon a structure badly built, and badly maintained'. The Board of Trade inquiry into the accident was headed by Henry Rothery, Wreck Commissioner, Colonel Yolland, Chief Inspector of Railways, and William Barlow, President of the Institution of Civil Engineers. Serious charges were levied against the quality of the iron castings, the standard of workmanship, and the slovenly policy of maintenance. Sir Thomas Bouch, the designer, came out of it very badly: 'For the faults of the design, he is entirely responsible. For those of construction, he is principally to blame... And for the faults of maintenance he is also principally, if not entirely, to blame'. The North British Railway Co. was

William George Armstrong (1810–1900), the father of hydraulic engineering.

43

also found 'not wholly free from blame for having allowed the trains to run through the high girders at a speed greatly in excess of that which General Hutchinson [one of the Board of Trade's railway inspectors] had suggested as the extreme limit'.

It emerged that there was no 'understood rule in the engineering profession regarding wind pressure in railway structures'. When Bouch had consulted Sir George Airy, the Astronomer Royal, in the early 1870s on the subject, Airy had said that the greatest wind pressure to which a plane surface like that of a bridge would be subjected on its whole length was 10lb. per sq. ft. Bouch applied this general advice to the Tay Bridge without making any allowance for its peculiarly exposed position. At the same time, he should have taken into consideration the requirements made elsewhere — 55lb. per sq. ft. in France, 50 in America. He could also have discovered that Benjamin Baker, later to be consulting engineer on the Forth Bridge, worked on 28lb. per sq. ft. The final outcome was the Board of Trade's ruling of 56lb. per sq. ft.

During construction of the Forth Bridge, wind pressure was carefully recorded using ordinary anemometers and a large wind gauge placed in a very exposed position. During a heavy gale in January 1884, the large gauge indicated a pressure of 35lb. per sq. ft. but nothing approaching this was ever registered again. Barry was so interested in the problem that he persuaded the Corporation to allow him to install a series of small self-recording wind gauges in the machinery chambers, on the roadway, and on the high-level walkways at Tower Bridge. On the bascules themselves, he had a huge wind

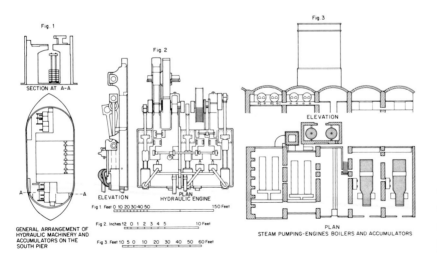

The machinery of Tower Bridge in the engine house and piers.

One of the steam pumping engines, the main source of power until mid-1971.

gauge with an area of 5,000 sq. ft. 'such as he supposed had never been heard of before'. In discussions following papers presented to the Institution of Civil Engineers in November 1896, Barry said that by comparing the records of the small wind gauges with the large, he was able to show that the falling off of pressure as surfaces increased in size 'was so marked, that the fallacy of any general principle of providing for a pressure of 56lb. per sq. ft. on surfaces independent of their size, would be a matter of proof in a short time'. He supposed that these findings might serve as a crumb of comfort to some 'who were responsible for structures which ought to have been blown down and carried away like straws long ago'.

Tower Bridge had two pumping engines and two sets of boilers in the engine house, and two sets of lines of pipes leading to the two sets of bascule-drive engines in the piers. The second set of machinery always had the water laid on but not necessarily under pressure.

Installed in the first two arches of the engine house were the four coal-burning double-furnace Lancashire boilers, each 7½ feet in diameter and 30 feet long. Two were in use at any one time, fired up to supply steam at 75lb. per sq. in. to the

45

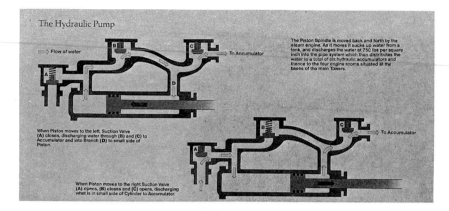

The Hydraulic Pump

Flow of water

To Accumulator

The Piston Spindle is moved back and forth by the steam engine. As it moves it sucks up water from a tank, and discharges the water at 750 lbs per square inch into the pipe system which then distributes the water to a total of six hydraulic accumulators and thence to the four engine rooms situated at the bases of the main Towers.

When Piston moves to the left, Suction Valve (A) closes, discharging water through (B) and (C) to Accumulator and into Branch (D) to small side of Piston.

When Piston moves to the right Suction Valve (A) opens, (B) closes and (C) opens, discharging what is in small side of Cylinder to Accumulator.

To Accumulator

Diagram of a hydraulic pump. The piston, moved backwards and forwards by the steam-engine, sucked up water from a tank and discharged it under pressure into the pipe system.

nearby pumping engine. Stokers kept the boilers fed with 20 tons of fuel a week. Coal was brought up river by barge and unloaded by hydraulic crane. It was then taken in small railway trucks into the store next to the boilers in the third arch. Once the floor had been filled, the trucks could be lifted by hydraulic hoist to an overhead line, running the length of the store, and the coal tipped into bunkers on either side.

The two magnificent steam pumping engines, resplendent in their green livery with red, black, and gold trim, occupied the fourth and fifth arches. One alone provided more than enough power to operate the bridge, pumping water under a pressure of 750lb. per sq. in. Barry wrote that this pressure was not unusual 'but its magnitude will be appreciated when we remember that in the boiler of a locomotive engine the steam pressure is usually not more than about one fifth of the above amount'.

The hydraulic pumps fed the water under pressure to the six accumulators, two in the accumulator house adjacent to the engine house, and two in each river pier. Their function was to maintain a constant pressure in the pipe system and to store surplus pump output at periods of low demand for immediate release the moment the request came to raise the bascules. Suffice it to say 'their capacity is ample for the most liberal demands of the hydraulic engine'.

The high-pressure water was conveyed by two 6-inch pipes from the accumulators to the lifting machinery. The pipes went along the Surrey fixed span to the south tower machinery chamber, up the steel columns of the south tower, over the top of the high-level walkways, and down the steel columns of the north tower to the pier. Once its energy was expended, the water ran back to the pumping engines through one

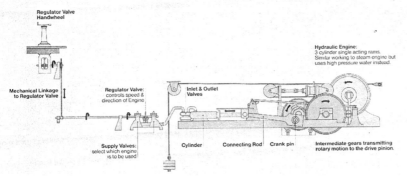

The bascule-drive engines operated in a similar manner to the steam-engines but used water under pressure instead of steam.

7-inch pipe. At any point where it was thought that changes in temperature or unequal loading of the spans might affect the pipes, special joints were provided that were capable of adjusting to the varying conditions. The mains were protected from frost by hot-water pipes laid alongside.

In each pier there were two machinery chambers, both housing a pair of bascule-drive engines. The smaller of the two could exert a pressure equal to a 17lb. wind and was intended for normal weather conditions. The larger, equal to a 39lb. wind, was for stormy weather. In exceptionally bad conditions, both could be used together to give sufficient power to raise and lower the bascules against the legendary 56lb. wind. Theoretically, the duplicate pair of engines followed up the work of the first and provided against breakdowns. In practice, it was never found necessary to use more than the two small engines.

To open the bridge, the high-pressure water passed to the hydraulic engines and drove the pistons, which turned cranks and moved a series of geared wheels. These were attached to the steel pinion shafts which ran the full width of the bridge and engaged with the toothed quadrants which turned to raise the bascules. The rate of movement at the far extremity was 2 feet per second — a moderate speed for an opening bridge. To raise the bascules took sixty seconds.

Each bascule weighs 1,200 tons and moves through a maximum arc of 83°. At the junction between the bascules are four locking bolts, one at the end of each main girder. Other safety precautions include resting blocks at the edges of the piers, in front of the main pivot shafts, and two pawls or tail locks which engage the undersides of each counterweight.

The bridge was remotely controlled from two cabins on the

east ends of the piers. Here drivers worked the operating and reversing levers, and the nose and tail locks. Interlocking gears fitted to the double row of levers, one for each end of the pier, made it impossible for them to carry out the operations in anything other than the correct sequence, or to commence any manoeuvre until the preceding one was completed. Connected to this gear were barriers for stopping the road traffic and signals for road and river traffic.

The drivers' actions were directed by the Head Watchman who checked that the bridge was clear before opening. Each driver could lift his bascule independently and it was usual for the south bascule to start to rise first, rapidly followed by the north bascule. A 'full' opening was normally reserved for a salute of honour to royalty, the Lord Mayor, and other distinguished persons. Under normal circumstances, each bascule was raised and lowered by one hydraulic engine. The other three were in gear and running idle, the water merely circulating through their cylinders and valves. But if he so wished, the driver could vary the power, change the engine, or switch power to the opposite end of the pier.

It is hard to imagine that every eventuality had not been covered. But just in case there was a complete breakdown, standby power was available from the mains of the London Hydraulic Power Company which had first begun supplying waterside and landside cranes, as well as dock gates and other heavy hydraulic machines, in 1884.

'South-east Control Cabin, Tower Bridge', 1973, mixed media, by Edna Lumb, 18in. × 33in.; one of a series of 25 paintings of the interior of Tower Bridge and its original machinery.

48

VI

A Day to Remember

The Opening of the Tower Bridge on Saturday was a picturesque and stately ceremonial, perfectly performed under the most favourable conditions...The decorations, both by land and water, were brilliant and profuse, the uniforms and robes splendid and varied, while the glorious sunshine brought out in full relief the many beauties of the great display and of the noble river which all true Englishmen love with a proud affection as the chiefest glory of their ancient capital.

(*The Times*, 2 July 1894)

SATURDAY, 30 JUNE 1894, was the perfect English summer day. For weeks, elaborate preparations had been under way for a spectacular opening ceremony. Invitations and tickets were designed and issued, bands and steamships specially booked, pavilions and marquees planned and erected. Everywhere was hung with bunting and flags, yards of crimson cloth, real and artificial flowers. The Mansion House was tastefully decorated with the City Arms and the Prince of Wales's feathers. The seven storeys of the Mazawattee Tea Warehouses on Tower Hill were nearly obliterated by the national colours, flags, and a huge sky sign which read 'Mazawattee Welcomes the Prince & Princess'. Every inch of space from Westminster to Blackfriars was occupied, the bridges and the Embankment packed with people. On the river, steamships, barges, and dumb barges jostled for position, while hundreds of watermen ferried out yet more visitors, ever hopeful of a good view.

Great tiers of seats had been erected on either side of the approaches to the bridge. As the minutes ticked by, continued *The Times*, 'the avenues of spectators grew more and more brilliant. Aldermen in scarlet and miniver, Common Councillors in mazarine and miniver, moved to and fro. The provincial

49

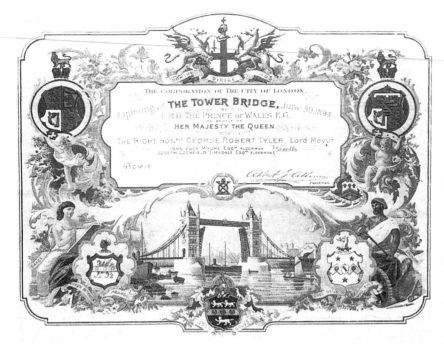

THE CORPORATION OF THE CITY OF LONDON.

Opening of THE TOWER BRIDGE, June 30, 1894.
BY
H R H THE PRINCE OF WALES K.G.
ON BEHALF OF
HER MAJESTY THE QUEEN.
THE RIGHT HON.ᴮᴸᴱ GEORGE ROBERT TYLER, Lord Mayor
JOHN VOCE MOORE ESQ.ᴺ ALDERMAN ⎫ Sheriffs
JOSEPH COCKFIELD DIMSDALE ESQ.ᴺ ALDERMAN ⎭

ADMIT

Ornamental card intended as a souvenir of the occasion, and sent out when a reply to the letter of invitation was received by the City Comptroller. The design was selected from thirteen competitive entries. The figures of Grace and Strength support an illustration of the bridge amidst the Royal Arms, the Arms of the Prince of Wales, the Arms of the Corporation, and the Armorial bearings of the Lord Mayor and Sheriffs.

mayors, including the Lord Mayor of Manchester, were conspicuous by their heavy gold chains of office. Here were ladies wearing the brightest of summer dresses, there were Orientals, with swarthy and impassive faces, with cool and flowing garments, in marked contrast to their fellow subjects of the West'. The crowds roared as they recognized distinguished visitors — Mr Asquith, Lord Spencer, the Bishops of London and Rochester, the Archbishop of Canterbury.

Their excitement mounted as members of the Royal family drew up in their carriages on the northern approach to await the arrival of the Prince and Princess of Wales. On the stroke of 12, the Royal procession appeared in sight, preceded by mounted police, a dazzling escort of guards, and carriages conveying the 'great engineer' and the Sheriffs, and the Lord Mayor. The bridge was opened to land traffic as the entire Royal cavalcade, headed by the Prince and Princess, moved majestically across to the Surrey side. The strains of the National Anthem played by the massed bands were just to be heard above the tumultuous applause.

The carriages then returned across the bridge and the Royal party descended at the opening ceremony pavilion. This was draped with pale pink and green muslin, and festooned with pink roses. Here the Princess of Wales could be seen wearing

The Mazawattee Tea Warehouses 'appropriately adorned for the extension of a hearty welcome to the Royal Visitors'.

51

The Royal cavalcade progressing across the bridge.

The opening ceremony pavilion, designed by Andrew Murray, the City Surveyor.

Opening the bridge to river traffic. The *St. James's Budget*, 6 July 1894, reported: 'His Royal Highness then turned the top of a large silver urn on the top of a pedestal, which communicated with the hydraulic machinery, and slowly, noiselessly, the great bascules forming the roadway of the bridge were seen to rise steadily into the air'. The cup, made by the Goldsmiths & Silversmiths Company, was presented to the Prince of Wales for performing the ceremony.

'a silk dress of the softest blue shade suffused with silver, with an underlying pattern similar to that of a very minute shepherd's plaid'. Her appearance won universal admiration.

In front of the Prince of Wales, a silver cup mounted on a specially designed pedestal had been rigged to communicate directly with the hydraulic machinery of the bridge. In reply to the Recorder's address on behalf of the Corporation, the Prince stepped forward, declared the bridge open for river traffic, and set the giant bascules in motion. The effect was remarkable. *The Times* eulogized: 'For a moment, the great crowd hushed in silence. Then in a deafening shout of applause, which soared, as only a British cheer can soar, above the thunder of the Tower guns, above the ringing notes of the trumpets, and above the wild din from the sirens and the whistles of the steamers, they gave vent to their admiration and delight at the marvel they had been privileged to see. They had indeed witnessed a spectacle not easily to be forgotten'. And they had also quite drowned the Benediction by the Bishop of London.

Through the bridge came HMS *Landrail*, decked from stem to stern with flags. She was followed by vessels representing the House of Commons, London County Council, Lloyd's, the Watermen's Company, and many other institutions. While the crowds enjoyed the river procession, notables and dignitaries were presented to their Royal Highnesses and the final leave-takings were made. The Royal party left from a tent on Tower Wharf to return to Westminster in the Victoria Steam Boat Association's vessel, the *Palm*. For the Princess of Wales, it was a busy day — she was due at the Home Arts and Industries Exhibition in the Royal Albert Hall at 4 p.m.

On the west side of the southern approach, two refreshment tents had been erected. The smaller gave breakfast and dinner to the Royal Naval Guard of Honour who had travelled up from Sheerness for the day. The larger provided a celebration meal for all the workmen employed under various contracts on the bridge, together with their wives or daughters. Some 1,200 attended, and pipes and tobacco and boxes of sweets were distributed as mementoes of the occasion. The cost to the Corporation was £272 8s. 4d.

For a few, there were medals to commemorate the event. For the majority, crêpe-paper handkerchiefs, the official programme, and Mazawattee's souvenir of the opening were available. The Corporation Librarian, Charles Welch, working against the clock, produced not only a small giveaway booklet for the day, but also a large-scale 'History of The Tower Bridge', the first copy of which was specially bound at the last minute and presented to the Prince of Wales.

The Times congratulated the City authorities on the consummate skill with which they had carried out the day's events. It praised the arrangements made for the ambulance stations and noted the kindness of two benefactors in providing schoolchildren on the south side with commemoration medals. Indeed, the paper found little to grumble about, save the London County Council's refusal to improve the tortuous southern approach. *The Graphic* and the *Illustrated London News*, both of which produced special supplements for the occasion, also extolled the bridge's virtues.

Gentlemen of the press had been invited to a private view of the bridge the Monday before the official opening. Once the euphoria of the day had passed, criticism of the opening was bound to come. Why had John Wolfe Barry received the small honour of Companion of the Bath when the chairman of the committee had been knighted? Why had George Stevenson not been mentioned in a single daily paper, and, what's more, not given a place on the dais? Why had the Strand been strewn with shell and gravel so that by 3 p.m. people were

The official programme, printed by the Bedford Programme Printing and Publishing Co. in the Strand, London. 'Programmes and Menus of Every Description for Balls, Soirées, Cricket and Football Clubs, Smoking Concerts, etc., Printed in good taste'.

C.48.4

SOUVENIR — JUNE. 30, 1894

Opening of The TOWER BRIDGE

By Their Royal Highnesses The PRINCE AND PRINCESS OF WALES

CITY ARMS, HIGH-LEVEL FOOTWAY.

MIDDLESEX ABUTMENT, WEST SIDE.

white with dust and freshly painted shop-fronts ruined?

Far more serious were the arguments raging over the bridge itself. The *Building News,* in its issue of 29 June 1894, was sorry that the labours of engineer and architect were so soon to be wasted. A see-saw bridge was a mistake and repeated raising and lowering of the bascules would be found tedious, then unnecessary. The bridge would become fixed 'which it might and should have been from the first, with the result that a million of money would have been saved'. On 27 July, it reported that Tower Bridge was of course a sham, 'as no real art can tolerate a casing'. However, the towers were preferable to huge skeletons of iron or steel which might have been 'prodigiously ugly'. In this *The Builder* did not agree: the towers were about 'as choice specimens of architectural gimcrack on a large scale as one could wish to see'. The naked steelwork would have revealed the structure and would at

A punning advertisement on the back of a promotional booklet.

56

least have been honest 'and we should have been relieved from the spectacle of many thousands spent on what is not the bridge at all, but an elaborate and costly make-believe'. *The Builder* felt so strongly that 'we decline to waste any plates in giving illustrations of the so-called architecture, but we give measured drawings of the only part of the structure that is worth anything, viz, the constructive steelwork'. It was, after all, simply a matter of opinion. The *Building News* found the upper galleries none too spacious, the lifts and staircases scarcely adequate, while *The Builder* regarded the stair as 'a very good and commodious one'.

The *Architect & Contract Reporter* felt that there was nothing very new or remarkable about the bridge apart from its scale. Londoners had certainly got a considerable amount of material for their money and there was nothing to equal the bascules anywhere in the world. It condemned the yellow brick engine house for 'being bald and ugly and obtrusive — a striking detraction from the beauty of the fine Gothic structure to which it is subsidiary'.

A sizeable Tower Bridge at the Crystal Palace, *c*.1894.

57

While some criticized, others admired. *The Times* hailed the bridge as 'one of the structural triumphs of this age of steel'. The *Engineering Review* found it undoubtedly the most successful structure to date for reconciling the requirements of shipping with those of pedestrians and vehicles. A visiting Frenchman had nothing but praise to offer: 'No other people know how to unite with the same harmonious force the cult of the past, the religion of tradition, to an unchecked love of progress and a lively and insatiable passion for the future'.

Whatever else, the bridge was there to stay and there were plenty ready to jump on the bandwagon. Owbridge's Lung Tonic quickly capitalized on the latest sight in town, while Beecham's accompanied a picture of the new bridge with their advertisement for 'the Bridge of Health...tried and found reliable for 50 years...a box of Beecham's Pills'. Cigarette cards, bookmarks, scraps, and postcards appeared in their hundreds, as well as more durable souvenir china. The Pavilion Theatre, Whitechapel, depicted 'the latest East End improvement, to wit, the Tower Bridge' on its new stage drop, and at Sydenham an impressive representation of the bridge arose before the Crystal Palace.

VII

Tower Bridge in Operation

Green to green and red to red — Perfect safety; go ahead.

(Rule of the Road, W.L. & M.A. Wyllie, *London to the Nore*, 1905)

THE FIRST TOWER Bridge Master, Lieutenant Bertie Cator, was appointed at an annual salary of £200 in April 1894, and took up his duties on 14 May, just six weeks before opening day. In the bridge's first year of operation, his staff raised the bascules 6,160 times and witnessed the daily crossing of 8,000 horse-drawn vehicles and 60,000 pedestrians.

From the very beginning, shipping had priority at Tower Bridge and any vessel with a mast or superstructure of 30 feet or over could request that the bridge be opened. The position of the bascules was signalled from four posts on the river piers. Semaphore arms dipped by day, and green lamps shone at night, when the bascules were raised. Red lights meant the bridge was closed, and as the Wyllies wrote: 'now and then, as some upward-bound vessel nears the bridge, the clang of the bell warns the traffic off, and the two great bascules rise grandly, the red lights turning into green'. In foggy weather, a gong was sounded. A tug was always in attendance to clear river traffic out of the way when the bascules were raised and to help any ship in difficulties.

Before Tower Bridge opened, it was calculated that an average of twenty-two vessels a day would need to have the bascules raised. Most would be sailing in the two hours before and the two hours after high water and it was quite likely that the bridge would have to be open for fifteen to twenty minutes if several ships went through one after another. The calculations were not far out: in the first year, the bridge opened seventeen times a day, in the second eighteen. It took on average six

A queue of horses and wagons waiting on the northern approach, c.1910.

minutes for the bridge to open and the longest delay was thirty-six minutes.

Hold-ups for horse-drawn traffic were no more than inconvenient since the approach roads were so easy. According to *The Times*, 'The gradients in the approaches to London Bridge are 1 in 21 on the north and 1 in 27 on the south side. The approach to the Tower Bridge is nearly level on the north and rises by no more than 1 in 40 to the south. What such a difference means to heavily-laden teams, particularly in our greasy London winters, nobody acquainted with horseflesh needs to be told'. Still, horses were kept stabled under the southern approach as standbys for animals that dropped dead in the traces. And the London County Council were very dilatory about fulfilling their share of the bargain and widening the southern approaches, though 'happily, it cannot lessen the benefit which the poorer classes whose daily work lies on the north side will enjoy from the improved means of access now given them to the cheapest quarters in the Southwark region'.

When the bascules were raised, pedestrians could either wait and watch at roadway level, or go to the top of the towers and cross via the high-level walkways. *The Builder* regarded the walkway as 'one of the most important features of the bridge, as it provides for uninterrupted communication in at least one form'. Two generous flights of stairs were provided in each tower, one for ascending and one for descending streams of people. Hydraulic lifts, capable of carrying twenty-five passengers each, could make twenty-five journeys up and down every hour but *The Builder* thought that 'for those who are not infirm or aged there is really no necessity for even the delay of waiting for the lift, as the climb upstairs is nothing very formidable'. Formidable or not, there were still 206 steps, laid with Mason's 'unwearable' non-slip treads by the Safety Tread Syndicate.

The towers and walkways were open from sunrise to sunset and were gas-lit as required. When the bridge opened, the *Building News* was sure that 'the lifts and staircases are scarcely adequate to the great passenger traffic that may be expected'. In fact, it was quite the reverse. In 1896, interruptions were proving so slight that it was still not thought to be necessary to open the lifts to the public. The walkways, commanding a fine view 140 feet above the Thames, were lovely for an Edwardian afternoon stroll, but were so under-utilized that they were shut from the beginning of 1910. Over twenty years later, in 1933, Mr Walter Jerrold in *London Described* lamented the loss of such a novel vantage point: 'It might well be made one of the recognised view points of London — a view point available to all on the payment of a small fee — for if...less extensive than from loftier points, the view is that one which most effectively affords pictures for the memory'. The Tower

A familiar sight at the turn of the century when the bascules were raised on average twenty times a day.

of London, the Monument, the dome of St. Paul's, 'the symbols of this City throughout the world', were there for all to see. And immediately below were the ever-busy wharves and the ceaseless stream of river traffic, described in great detail by Sir Walter Besant in *East London*, 1901: 'the stately East and West Indiamen, the black collier, the brig and the brigantine and the schooner, the Dutch galliot, the three-masted Norwegian, the coaster, and the multitudinous smaller craft — the sailing barge, the oyster boat, the smack, the pinnace, the snow, the yacht, the lugger, the hog boat, the ketch, the hoy, the lighter, and the wherries, and always ships dropping down the river with the ebb, or making their slow way up the river with the flow'.

In the 1890s, Tower Bridge had an operating staff of eighty including the Bridge Master and his team, and the Resident Engineer and his workforce. Either the Bridge Master or his deputy was on duty day and night, together with engine-drivers, watchmen, signalmen, firemen, and eight constables from the City police. In 1894, Armstrongs provided fifty-seven men to work on the hydraulic machinery, as well as all the coal, oils, waste, and miscellaneous stores. The Engineer dealt with everything from reflooring and repainting the bridge to erecting flagstaffs and making good damage caused by ships colliding with the piers. In addition, there was a maintenance staff of up to thirty men. Their workshops, adjacent to the engine house, were finished in the middle of 1895, and housed blacksmiths, carpenters, and plumbers on the ground floor, and machine shops above. Few jobs on the bridge were beyond the capabilities of these men and their equipment. The various moving parts of the steam and bascule-drive engines were under continuous overhaul, while steam and water valves required regular maintenance. Spare parts, special tools, and gauges were manufactured in the machine shop and by the blacksmiths. Pipework and gas-light fittings were assembled, repaired, and overhauled by the plumbers. The blacksmiths also cared for the bridge's horses.

The Bridge Master and the Resident Engineer both lived on site, in the abutment towers. Hydraulic pumps in the machinery chambers of the piers delivered water to their living quarters. In 1912, the Bridge Master was able to move to superior accommodation, the Tower Bridge Residence on the southern approach. For some lucky workers, there were flats at Wapping.

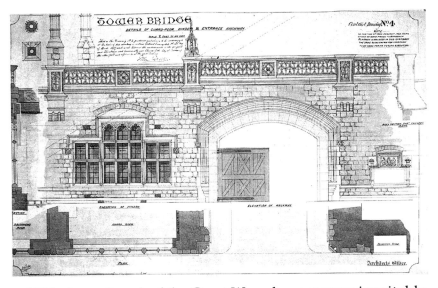

Details of the guardroom window and entrance archway. The Memorial Stone is drawn on the right and can be seen at the base of the western elevation of the north abutment on the Tower waterfront.

With the outbreak of the Great War, changes were inevitable. Operating staff now had to do some of the maintenance work and disabled soldiers and sailors filled temporary vacancies. In 1917, John Gass, the Superintending Engineer, no longer deemed it necessary for staff to have been sailors because 'many steady men, with ordinary intelligence and good eyesight, would be quite able to fill the post of either watchman or signalman after a little instruction'. Moves were afoot for a single principal officer rather than both a Bridge Master and an Engineer and 'there cannot be the least doubt that the official should be an Engineer with a thorough knowledge (theoretical and practical) of machinery, for on this, the successful working of the bridge depends'.

The only parts of the bridge not devoted to bridge activities were the arches under the northern approach, which were on permanent loan to the Tower of London garrison. Rather than let the northern approach interfere with important wharf property, the military authorities agreed to give up a small part of the Tower Ditch. In return, they not only stipulated that the architecture of the bridge should be in keeping, but they also asked that the 'new works should be made suitable for the mounting of guns and for military occupation'. Though this never happened, a guardroom and uniform store were built into the archway nearest to the abutment tower. The cast-iron chimney from the guardhouse is the odd man out in the line of cast-iron lamps placed at intervals along the approach road parapet.

63

'Rescued!' From Cassell's *Living London*, 1901.

Next door to the guardroom, an unfilled archway provided a through passage under the approach road, and led to Dead Man's Hole. This sinister spot was used as a mortuary for bodies retrieved from the river until they could be removed for burial. Popular myth has it that the upper walkways of the bridge were shut because of the number of attempted suicides, but it was simply not possible to get out through the boarding and metal tracery. If the Incident Books are to be believed, it was from bascule level that the poor unfortunates jumped, many to be rescued by the Thames River Police.

But life on the bridge was mostly routine. Occasionally vessels struck the bascules with masts and funnels, went into the piers, or collided with each other. Horses died, cars and motor vans skidded. Lamp standards got broken and masonry was known to fall. And there was the usual chapter of human mishaps. But these were always the exceptions and throughout the bridge continued to operate effortlessly and faultlessly.

VIII

Round and About the Bridge

He [Frank McClean] missed Tower Bridge. You shouldn't.
Nowadays a £2 ticket is all you'll need.

(Poster advertisement, 1986)

ON 10 AUGUST 1912, Frank McClean stole a Frenchman's thunder when he became the first man to fly through Tower Bridge. Reporters and photographers from the *Daily Mail* were all lined up to record the historic flight of the famous Lieutenant de Conneau up the course of the Thames through the City of London to a reception at Carmelite House. But while de Conneau was delayed in Boulogne with engine trouble, McClean left the Isle of Sheppey, bound for Westminster, in his Short pusher biplane. Unable to climb above the top of Tower Bridge, he amazed the waiting spectators by taking the only alternative route — between the bascules and the high-level walkways. The police forbade him to repeat his performance on the return journey.

Tower Bridge is more than the scene of deeds of daring. Its bascules have been raised to honour the living, mourn the dead, and allow the passage of some very unlikely craft. It has led a charmed existence, escaping virtually unscathed in the two World Wars and suffering mostly insignificant wear and tear.

In the early days of the Great War, *The Graphic* and the *Illustrated London News* were at pains to show that business continued as usual on the busy Thames. In September 1915, the first Zeppelin to fly over the City dropped a bomb near the Guildhall, heralding the start of a series of nightly raids on London. Taking the 'Thames Bridge' as a symbol, German propaganda depicted fate drawing nigh, hovering over the walkways and open bascules. Fortunately, the bridge remained unharmed.

During the 1930s, a certain amount of refurbishment was undertaken at the bridge, both above and below water. In 1932, the roadway surface was replaced by the Improved Wood Paving Company. The wood-block paving of the carriageway was a constant problem. Water continually permeated the surface, causing swelling of the timber and minor eruptions which had to be patched or repaved. In the same year, the City authorities were obliged to commit an 'offence' at Tower Bridge — the dumping of refuse to fill deep cavities in the river bed close to the foundations. In 1934, the wooden floor in the pumping engine room was replaced by steel floor plates and two years later a third engine was installed by Messrs Vickers-Armstrongs Ltd. Work on the high-level walkways started with the partial opening up of the zinc roof in preparation for painting. Much of the cast-iron panelling was found to be rusty and unsafe and it was taken down and ingloriously sold for scrap, making £220 12s. In 1938, the signalling system, gongs, indicators, and intercommunicating telephones were reported to be worn out, but their updating had to wait until after the war.

In 1939, the control cabins were sheathed with steel plating and sand-bagged as precautionary measures. When the Blitz began, it took its toll at Tower Bridge, breaking windows and roof slates, and knocking off chunks of granite. On 16 April 1941, a bomb exploded damaging the south shore span and injuring five people with flying glass and debris. The staff remained but there was very little traffic on the river. The activities of the attending tug were curtailed and one was sunk by a doodlebug in 1944. The last air raid on the City came in March 1945. By then, the area to the north-east of St. Paul's lay devastated, there had been seventeen attacks on the Houses of Parliament, and the Tower of London had suffered fifteen direct hits.

It was in an unsolicited report to the Bridge House Estates Committee in November 1943 that W.F.C. Holden, the architect to the National Provincial Bank, put forward his proposal for a glass-encased Tower Bridge. His crystal superstructure would obviate the need to repair war damage because 'it would not then be necessary to expend large sums of money in restoring and replacing decayed portions and in continually repainting this enormous structure the life of which — however much is spent — cannot be extended indefinitely'. Holden retained the approximate form and outline of the

Frank McClean flying through Tower Bridge. He then skimmed through all the remaining bridges to Westminster at just above water level.

Holden's Crystal Tower Bridge, 1943. The design incorporated 200,000 sq. ft. of light airy office space and would have elicited a considerable annual revenue for the Bridge House Estates Trust.

existing bridge 'without which the view of the Pool...would be definitely impoverished', and envisaged his design as a focus for post-war planning in the vicinity. The Bridge House Estates Committee entertained him to lunch and referred his scheme to their consulting engineers. But the Crystal Tower Bridge was never to be, and soon after the war, damage was made good. Bill Brookman, helped by his son Leslie, replaced the slate roofs, hanging 48 tons of slate on 55,000 copper nails. The job ran in the family since Bill's father had laid the original slates over half a century earlier.

On 30 December 1952, a double-decker bus jumped a 3-foot gap when the northern bascule began to rise before the road traffic had cleared the bridge. Its driver, Albert Gunton, told *The Times:* 'I had to keep going, otherwise we should have been in the water. I suddenly saw the road in front of me appeared to be sinking. In fact, the bus was being lifted by one half of the bridge. The other half was stationary as the bus crashed on to it on four wheels'. The last recorded occasion when a vehicle had been on the bridge when the bascules started to move was in 1943. A van driver had failed to see the warning lights, had driven on, and had skidded into the rising south bascule.

Like much of the capital, Tower Bridge was specially lit for the Coronation of Her Majesty the Queen in June 1953. A year later, following the Royal World Tour, the bascules were raised for the triumphant return of the Royal Yacht *Britannia* and

The flypast at the funeral of Sir Winston Churchill, 1965.

68

Artist's impression —
there is no photograph
— of the No. 78
Shoreditch-to-Dulwich
bus astride the
bascules. The bus
landed on its rear
wheels with a great
jolt, injuring the driver,
conductor, and eight
passengers.

Unloading in the Pool of London, December 1949.

the walkways bore a personal message for the Queen — WELCOME HOME. In the 1960s, national heroes were mourned and cheered. For the funeral of Sir Winston Churchill, on 10 January 1965, dockside cranes in the Upper Pool were dipped in salute. In July 1967, the bascules were raised to hail Sir Francis Chichester, the famous round-the-world solo yachtsman, in *Gypsy Moth IV*.

Traffic in the London Docks and the Pool after the Second World War was a mere shadow of its former self. At the end of the nineteenth century, five dock systems extended over 3,000 acres with 36 miles of quay and 665 acres of dock basin. A policy of modernization, instituted by the newly created Port of London Authority in 1909, increased prosperity until the Blitz, when the docks and East London were bombed nightly for two months. Despite heavy wartime damage, the docks made a remarkable recovery. By 1959, the Port of London Authority had virtually finished reconstruction, tonnage was over 50 million annually, and the dock system was handling one-third of Britain's seaborne trade. The revival continued until the mid-1960s when the docks went into rapid and terminal decline.

The life of Tower Bridge as a moving bridge has always been inextricably linked with the volume of traffic on the Thames. As the 1960s slipped by, the number of ships seeking passage to the Upper Pool fell dramatically. From April 1962, any ship's captain wanting the bascules raised had to give twenty-four hours' notice. It began to look as if the days of the opening Tower Bridge were numbered.

70

IX

Open Again, 1982

*It is one of the most difficult of Britain's larger white elephants
but still comparable with the Eiffel Tower, the Leaning Tower
of Pisa, and even, perhaps, the Taj Mahal. It is a traffic
crossing whose usefulness is running out. But it is also a
listed monument that has appeared in millions of photographs
and tourist guides all over the world.*

(*The Scotsman*, 3 August 1977)

SINCE 1976, TOWER Bridge has been operated by electrical
power taken from the London Electricity Board's supply on
the south bank. Maintaining the Victorian hydraulic engines
in working order was a gross indulgence in view of the
greatly reduced number of ships requiring the bascules to be
raised. The change-over coincided with the contemplation of
new uses for the bridge as well as with mounting concern
over its condition.

The modernization of the machinery had been mooted as
long ago as 1917. Suggestions ranged from removing the whole
hydraulic system and driving all machinery by electrical power
to using the Hydraulic Power Company to drive the existing
machinery, or the Electric Power Company to supply elec-
trically driven pumping engines. Cruttwell, Wolfe-Barry's
former resident engineer, and one of the authors of the report,
conferred with John Gass, the Superintending Engineer of the
bridge, and both were of the opinion that the system then in
operation was the best. Gass's opinion was based on long-
standing experience. As foreman fitter with Armstrongs, he
had installed and erected the machinery, and had then joined
the Tower Bridge staff in 1894.

Further reports in 1925 and 1931 were still against any
change. In 1946, John Buchanan, the then Superintending

Engineer, was still against any change. 'Consider this original plant which has given you 52 years of well-nigh trouble free service and operated the bascules nearly 300,000 times. Could any electrical firm or expert guarantee a similar period of service with [an] electrical driving mechanism? I am sure they could not'. There was always the risk of power cuts stopping the bridge at critical moments, and the generation of electrical power was out of the question because of capital costs and the complete change in the operating skills required.

In September 1970, the Court of Common Council of the Corporation agreed to the policy of retaining Tower Bridge as an opening bridge, as opposed to leaving the bascules permanently in the lowered position. Parliamentary powers were to be sought for early modernization of the machinery and improvements to the structure. The following year, an impassioned letter to *The Times* deplored the City's decision to replace 'the remarkable mechanism, which is the most perfect example of integrated hydraulic power in the world'. The writer begged that the bridge be 'designated a museum of industrial archaeology, and the machinery kept intact, and made available to the public'.

The tender by Cleveland Bridge & Engineering Co. Ltd. for installing two electrical units at each corner of Tower Bridge was accepted in 1972. History repeated itself since the units

Inside one of the four machinery rooms. The electric motor (bottom centre) drives the oil pump on the right. High-pressure oil drives motors connected to the original rack pinion shafts and when these rotate, the bascules rise or fall.

Removing the 1936 steam pumping engine. Through the efforts of Dr R.N. Francis, this engine was found a new home at the Forncett Industrial Steam Museum, Forncett St. Mary, near Norwich.

provide stand-by power 100 per cent in excess of that normally required to raise the bascules. Installation entailed the removal of much of the original hydraulic plant and pipework but it was decided to retain two steam pumping engines and four bascule-drive engines on a non-operational basis. The Corporation, taking a leaf from its London Bridge notebook, hit on the idea of selling the remaining machinery, provoking headlines like 'Tower power goes up for sale!' and 'Tower Bridge not for sale — but the machinery is!'

So that the bridge might remain operational while the new machinery was installed, the work was divided into two stages. The existing control cabins and drive machinery on the downstream side were retained to operate the bridge while the machinery in the two upstream plant rooms was removed and the new equipment installed. The south-west watchman's cabin was made into a control cabin. New road and pedestrian gates were installed together with closed-circuit television and a public address system. Test openings were made and a trial period of operation undertaken with the old equipment acting as a stand-by. The second stage involved the removal of all the remaining machinery and the installation of another set of replacements. A further control desk was installed in the north-east cabin so that the bridge could now be operated from the side from which the ship was approaching.

Spare parts for the old machinery were purpose-made and, as a result, operating and maintenance costs were high. The replacement machinery was designed around standardized components and could be operated by only one person. Consequently, less than a dozen full-time staff were required to man the bridge and former no-go areas, barred for safety and operational reasons, now became accessible. Suggestions for admitting tourists to the bridge, first put forward in 1972, could now be seriously entertained. The architects, Holford Associates, were invited to devise a scheme which would encourage public interest in the structure and allow access to as many parts as possible. Mott, Hay & Anderson, consultant engineers, were to deal with any structural alterations arising from their proposals and Kenneth R. Kensall & Partners were appointed quantity surveyors. As reported in the Common Council minutes, both the architects and Robin Wade Design Associates, exhibition consultants, were acutely aware of the need 'to alter the character of the inside as little as is consistent with the work of providing smooth and attractive circulation for visitors' and that 'great attention to detail and sympathetic handling in the design of crowd control barriers, internal lighting and in redecoration' would be necessary. Nor was the outside appearance of the bridge forgotten: Holfords were to preserve its external aspect as far as possible.

The repainting of Tower Bridge's ironwork in patriotic red, white, and blue began in October 1976. A sarcastic reader commented in *The Times* that the Tower of London would be made to look shoddy by comparison and that, while they were at it, the authorities should consider Snowcemming Buckingham Palace and giving Nelson's Column a coat of Day-glo. The City of London stoutly defended its colour choice, pointing out that 'red, white, and blue' was an oversimplification, that there were 'several different blues involved, plus some greys and reds', and anyway anything was an improvement on the old battleship grey.

At the same time, fears were being voiced about the 10,000 commercial vehicles thundering across the bridge every day. Juggernauts and container lorries, weighing in at over 30 tons, were a far cry from the 7-ton Victorian drays, travelling at 3 m.p.h., for which the bridge had been built. There was no imminent danger of collapse, but the possibilities of metal fatigue and loosening of the cladding led the Greater London

The coat of arms of the City of London awaits lift-off to one of the high-level walkways. The grp finials in the foreground are two of the eight reinstated on the corner pinnacles of the main towers to restore the silhouette of the bridge. The original massive stone crosses, linked to the apex of the pinnacles by only a short metal dowel, had been removed during the war for safety reasons.

Council to impose a 5-ton unladen lorry limit at the end of January 1979. Close examination of the stonework became feasible when scaffolding was erected for cleaning and refurbishment purposes. A remarkably small number of defects were found to have been caused by differential movement of the structural framework and the masonry cladding, but years of erosion and chemical attack had taken a severe toll of the fabric, and a force of up to eighteen masons was at times engaged on site to replace Portland stone and granite. In the two main towers, Goddard & Gibbs, stained glass artists and craftsmen, removed, rebuilt, or repaired all the glass in the windows. They reused as much original glass as possible, replacing missing panes with their 'antique' hand-made glass.

Reopening the walkways for public use required Parliamentary approval. The roofs were reinstated in aluminium, the sides glazed for weather protection, and an external walkway provided for maintenance purposes. The missing cast-iron ornamentation, the last of which was taken down in 1941, was replaced with glass reinforced plastic (grp) in all its original detail but at a fraction of its original weight.

Final touches were added by helicopter. Gilded grp finials were lowered into position on the rooftops of the main towers on a bright but blustery Sunday morning. On the same occasion, coats of arms of the City of London and emblems of the Bridge House Estates, once again moulded in grp, were carefully reinstalled on the walkways. Tower Bridge was thus restored to its former glory, renovated for five times its original price.

Today, visitors to the bridge can ascend the north tower, cross the high-level walkways, and go down the south tower to the Tower Bridge Museum, formerly the engine house. The stout-hearted use the original double staircases, while for those less sound in wind and limb, new lifts have replaced the old hydraulic ones. Landings provide welcome resting points and lofty spaces for exhibitions of historical material. In the south tower, part of the ceiling has been removed to reveal the roof space soaring up to support the restored roof finial, 235 feet above the river. From the walkways, visitors may once again enjoy spectacular views up and down the Thames. In the museum, they can inspect the boilers and steam pumping engines, the accumulators, and one of the bascule-drive engines, taken from the chamber at the west end of the south pier and reconstructed. Animated diagrams, a video film, a model, and reconstructed mechanisms explain the complete workings of the bridge.

On 30 June 1982 — eighty-eight years to the day since the original opening — Tower Bridge was opened once more to the public by the Right Honourable the Lord Mayor Sir Christopher Leaver. The mayoral party passed under the raised bascules of Tower Bridge bound for St. Katharine Dock in the Thames barge *Lady Daphne*. As the group walked back along the north bank of the river towards the bridge, the coastal minesweeper HMS *Pollington* and the clipper ships *Marques* and *Inca* passed upstream to the Upper Pool and the band of the Honourable Artillery Company struck up with 'Maybe It's Because I'm A Londoner'. The Bridge Master, arrayed in Victorian costume, greeted the Lord Mayor and conducted him to the east walkway for the unveiling of an official plaque. As the walkways and museum were declared open to the public, 1,000 balloons, each with a free entry ticket attached, were launched from the high-level walkways to mark the day's event.

Amongst the honoured guests was Miss Beatrice Quick, now in her nineties, and remarkable for her previous attendance at the 1894 opening. She recalled how when she was 4 her father, working as an engineer on the construction, had made sure that she was 'the first little girl to cross Tower Bridge from one side to the other'.

The Lord Mayor, accompanied by the Bridge Master, Lieutenant-Commander Anthony Rabbit, and Miss Beatrice Quick, on opening day.

A New View from the Bridge

This great structure [Tower Bridge] still dominates its sur-
roundings and provides a splendid western gateway to Dock-
lands as well as an architectural frame to the City and
central London.

(London Docklands Development Corporation,
Docklands Heritage, 1987)

DURING THE 1960s and 1970s, the working port of London moved progressively downstream, leaving in its wake empty docks, abandoned warehouses, and acres of derelict land. Between 1965 and 1975, 150,000 jobs were lost and a way of life all but vanished. The docks were too far upstream for the size of modern vessels, the new cargo-handling techniques, and the growing oil traffic. When the last two dock systems in the Greater London area — the West India and Millwall Docks and the Royal Group of Docks — closed in 1980 and 1981 respectively, business was concentrated at Tilbury Dock and the oil terminals, twenty miles and more down river.

What might be done with the eight square miles of deserted dockland, close to the heart of London, was a continuing challenge to planners and politicians throughout the 1970s. In 1981, the London Docklands Development Corporation (LDDC) was charged with the regeneration of this inner city area, the magnitude of which was unsurpassed in Europe. As statutorily defined, Docklands is the size of the West End and the City of London put together and stretches from Tower Bridge to Beckton on the north side of the river, and from London Bridge to Deptford on the south. The choice of Tower Bridge as the LDDC's logo recognized the bridge's historic position as the western gateway of the old docks.

The location of the new London City Airport in the Royals has now opened up the eastern end of Docklands as a gateway to Western Europe and the rest of Britain. Not far to the east, at Gallions Reach, is the site of the proposed Great East London River Crossing. The high-level suspension bridge — London's eighteenth bridge — will cross the Thames from Beckton to Thamesmead with link roads north to the A13 and M11, and south to the A2. A bridge east of Tower Bridge was first considered in the 1960s when an alternative crossing had to be found for heavy lorries. Plans were drawn up for the 'Pool of London Route', with a bridge a quarter of a mile east of Tower Bridge, linking Thomas More Street to St. Saviour's Dock as part of London's inner ring road system. The passage of time and the revitalization of Docklands have led to the relocation of this crossing six miles downstream. A century on from the construction of Tower Bridge, the new bridge is expected to have similar popular appeal and to become, in the words of the LDDC, 'as much a tourist attraction as that other great feat of 20th century engineering, the Thames Barrier'.

Great efforts are being made to preserve the architectural and industrial heritage of Docklands, from warehouses and dock and riverside structures to hydraulic pumping stations, shipbuilding yards, and street furniture. The Museum in Docklands has assembled vast collections relating to the working river, including traditional Thames craft, cargo-handling equipment, and material from the many ancillary trades associated with the docks. Equally significant are the photographs, memorabilia, and reminiscences of the steve-dores and dockers, their wives and families.

For the men who worked the river, the traditional method of handling cargoes, opening and closing lock gates, moving

Flying the flag: the logo of the London Docklands Development Corporation takes graphic licence with the surmounting tracery of the main towers.

London Docklands, covering the four main development areas — Wapping, the Isle of Dogs, the Royal Docks, and the Surrey Docks.

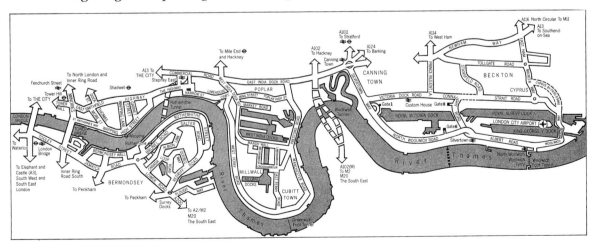

swing bridges, and loading trucks was hard manual labour. In the second half of the nineteenth century, the application of hydraulic power to all these activities was of major importance. High on the list of manufacturers of hydraulic machinery was of course Armstrongs, but other firms in Leeds, Kilmarnock, Carlisle, Gateshead, and Chester left their mark on Docklands, as did the local East Ferry Road Engineering Works Co. Ltd.

Tower Bridge stands at the head of, and has played a part in, this area of outstanding maritime and historic interest. The bridge itself falls within two conservation areas which meet at the intersection of the bascules. The northern side lies in the Tower Conservation Area which includes the Tower of London, the Mint, and the St. Katharine Docks. The docks, which opened in 1828, consisted of two principal basins, the East and the West. Here the engineer Thomas Telford pioneered the use of warehouses constructed right up to the water's edge. Goods could be taken straight from ship to warehouse without double handling in a transit shed. Sadly, many of these fine warehouses were destroyed in 1940, or have suffered subsequent demolition. Since the closure of the docks in 1968, the area has been redeveloped as an attractive and popular haven for different types of craft, including cabin cruisers, yachts, and Thames barges, as well as historic vessels.

The southern portion of the bridge is part of the Tower Bridge Conservation Area which includes the former main Courage's Brewery, immediately east of the bridge. The large group of warehouse buildings, known as Butler's Wharf, falls in the Tower Bridge and adjoining St. Saviour's Dock Conservation Areas. The wharf was the largest on the Thames when it was completed in 1873 and the original building, now undergoing careful renovation, features prominently in

Artist's impression of the proposed bridge which will cross the Thames at a point midway between the Blackwall and Dartford Tunnels.

the view from Tower Bridge and the St. Katharine Docks. The complex of warehouses rises up on the bank of the Thames, enclosing narrow streets, and creating a great sense of drama. Most striking of the streets is the canyon-like Shad Thames, where the warehouses are connected by lattice iron bridges at all levels. Current proposals for Butler's Wharf are for a mixed development of homes, offices, shops and workshops, and cultural and leisure facilities. The main warehouses will be converted or refurbished and the integration of new buildings is planned.

The retention of the street atmosphere and dockland aspect of this area is particularly important as the Tower Bridge and St. Saviour's Dock Conservation Areas, and the area from

The restored Ivory House, St. Katharine Docks, January 1986.

Landing ginger at Butler's Wharf, *c.* 1900. Goods were transferred to the towering warehouses and the smell of spices still lingers in the narrow streets.

Aerial view looking west towards the City of London, December 1986.

Tooley Street to London Bridge, have been described as the only parts of London in which the Victorian character survives as a significant entity. Extending west from St. Saviour's Dock, Tooley Street connects Tower Bridge and London Bridge and links the narrow access roads which served the wharves along the Bermondsey river front. A series of mixed commercial and residential developments, London Bridge City, will eventually stretch along this part of the Thames between the two historic bridges. Already refurbished at the west end of Tooley Street are Emblem House and Chamberlain's Wharf as a private hospital, and Hay's Dock with its glazed 'Galleria'.

To the north-west of Tower Bridge, the Tower of London stands immutable. In every other direction, the view from the bridge is one of progress and change. A new landscape is emerging, as much in response to twentieth-century needs as Tower Bridge was to nineteenth-century demands. London's most famous gateway bridges the gap between old and new: may its place in our affections never diminish.

Notes on Sources

General Information

The most comprehensive collection of reference material for Tower Bridge is in the Corporation of London Records Office and the Guildhall Library. This includes contract drawings, plans, and sections; inventories, ledgers, electrification reports, and miscellaneous papers; and ephemera, prints, and photographs. Particularly useful are:

Minutes of Evidence to the House of Commons Select Committee on the Corporation of London Tower Bridge Bill, 1884–5

Reports of the Bridge House Estates Committee to the Court of Common Council

Other principal sources of information are the Museum of London, the Institution of Civil Engineers, and the British Library Newspaper Library.

Select Bibliography

Sir William Arrol & Co. Ltd., *Bridges, Structural Steel Work & Mechanical Engineering Productions* (published for private circulation by *Engineering*, 1909)

The Corporation of London (Tower Bridge) Act, 1885 (48 and 49 Vic, cap. cxcv)

Theo Crosby, *The Necessary Monument* (London, Studio Vista, 1970)

Dockland, An illustrated historical survey of life and work in East London (London, North East London Polytechnic/Greater London Council, 1986)

Docklands Heritage, Conservation and Regeneration in London Docklands (London, London Docklands Development Corporation, 1987)

The Tower Bridge, A Lecture by John Wolfe Barry (London, Boot, Son & Carpenter, 1894)

J.E. Tuit, *The Tower Bridge, its History and Construction, from the Date of the Earliest Project to the Present Time* (London, *The Engineer*, 1894)

Charles Welch, *History of The Tower Bridge* (London, Smith, Elder & Co., 1894)

NEWSPAPERS AND PERIODICALS

Contemporary descriptions of the progress of construction, and accounts of the opening, are to be found in:

The Architect
Architect & Contract Reporter
The Builder
Building News
The Engineer
Engineering
Engineering Review
The Graphic
Illustrated London News
Minutes of Proceedings of the Institution of Civil Engineers
St. James's Budget
The Times

SOURCES OF ILLUSTRATIONS

The author and publisher would like to thank the following for permission to reproduce illustrations in the book:

Sir William Arrol-NEI Thompson Ltd., pp. 23, 24, and 25; Barnaby's Picture Library, p. 45; BBC Hulton Picture Library, pp. 2, 28, 40, 60, 61, and 70; Bridgeman Art Library, London, front cover; Butlers Wharf Ltd., p. 82 (top); Corporation of London Records Office, pp. 14 (top), 52 (below), 63, 68, and back cover; Crystal Palace Foundation, p. 57; Department of Transport, p. 80; John Gay, frontispiece; Guildhall Library, City of London, pp. 3 (top), 5, 10, 11, 12, 13, 20, 31, 39, 51, and 55; Institution of Civil Engineers, p. 44; London Docklands Development Corporation, pp. 79, 81, and 82 (bottom); Edna Lumb, p. 48; Mansell Collection, pp. 43, 52 (above), and 53; Museum of London, pp. 36 and 64; Robert Opie Collection, pp. 6 and 56; Mrs J.F. Peach, pp. 22 (left) and 38; from the exhibitions on Tower Bridge, pp. 7, 42, 50, 67, and 75; University Librarian, University of Bristol, p. 17; Albert Yee, p. 77.